This book is published strictly for historical purposes.
The Naval and Military Press Ltd
expressly bears no responsibility or liability of any type,
to any first, second or third party, for any harm,
injury or loss whatsoever.

WAR DEPARTMENT   OFFICE OF THE CHIEF OF STAFF

MANUAL OF
Physical Training

FOR USE IN THE

UNITED STATES ARMY

The Naval & Military Press Ltd

Published by

The Naval & Military Press Ltd
Unit 5 Riverside, Brambleside
Bellbrook Industrial Estate
Uckfield, East Sussex
TN22 1QQ England

Tel: +44 (0)1825 749494

www.naval-military-press.com
www.nmarchive.com

*In reprinting in facsimile from the original, any imperfections are inevitably reproduced
and the quality may fall short of modern type and cartographic standards.*

WAR DEPARTMENT,
Document No. 436.
Office of the Chief of Staff

WAR DEPARTMENT,
OFFICE OF THE CHIEF OF STAFF,
Washington, February 20, 1914.

The following Manual of Physical Training, prepared by a board of officers consisting of Lieut. Col. Fred W. Sladen, United States Army; Capt. Herman J. Koehler, United States Army; and First Lieut. Philip Mathews, Coast Artillery Corps, is published for the information and government of the Regular Army and the Organized Militia of the United States.

In the preparation of this Manual the demands of the service and the facilities to meet these demands were constantly kept in mind.

The board also endeavored to treat the subject in a manner that would insure its successful application by all officers, thus making it possible to place this part of the soldiers' training upon a permanent and uniform basis.

There is nothing in the education of the soldier of more vital importance than this, and while considerable has been accomplished by some commands in this respect in the past it has, owing to the absence of any well-defined authorized method of procedure, lacked system and uniformity, without which the benefits to the service in general will continue to remain a negligible quantity.

The physical training of the enlisted men should, therefore, be carried out in accordance with the instructions laid down herein.

Officers to whom this work is intrusted will find the material the Manual affords and its arrangement more than ample to meet any condition. While a strict adherence to the text or the manner of its application is not necessarily to be insisted upon, departures from it that are at variance with its methods generally should not be encouraged.

By order of the Secretary of War:

LEONARD WOOD,
Major General, Chief of Staff.

THE OBJECT AND SCOPE OF PHYSICAL TRAINING IN THE SERVICE.

OBJECT.

The objects which a course in physical training in the service aim to attain are the development of the physical attributes of every individual to the fullest extent of his possibilities.

These, in order of their importance, may be summed up as follows:
  (a) General health and bodily vigor.
  (b) Muscular strength and endurance.
  (c) Self-reliance.
  (d) Smartness, activity, and precision.

It is upon the first of these, *health* and *bodily vigor*, that the development of all the other qualities so essential in a soldier are dependent, and for that reason the maintenance of *robust health* and the development of *organic vigor* should be considered the primary object of this training.

The tendency of the age is to treat all conditions of health from a pathological standpoint; and while much has been accomplished in the way of increasing the resistive powers of the human organism against the inroads of disease by means of inoculation and other methods of prevention, the development of the inherent power of resistance, which every individual possesses in a greater or lesser degree by means of natural physiological methods, has been much neglected.

It is not sufficient, however, for a soldier to be healthy; his profession demands that he possess more than the average amount of muscular strength and endurance in addition to good health, in order that he may be ready to exchange the comparative comforts of barrack life for the hardships of field service at any moment without diminishing his effectiveness. Hence, the preparatory training he receives must contain those elements that will enable him to do so successfully.

With robust health as a basis and with the knowledge that he is the possessor of more than average strength and endurance, he must be taught how to value the former and how to use the latter to the best advantage. By doing so he will unwittingly develop self-reliance, which, after all, is a physical quality, as it induces men to dare because of the consciousness to do.

Smartness, activity, and precision are the physical expressions of mental activity. All are essential soldierly qualities, as they make for self-respect, neatness, and grace, which combined spell discipline. Precision and exactitude should therefore always be insisted upon in the performance of all exercises prescribed.

In the endeavor to attain the objects referred to above the soldier will be the recipient of a course of training that can not fail to develop him harmoniously, and the liability of developing one portion of his body at the expense of another will be obviated.

SCOPE.

The material at the disposal of instructors embraces:
 1. Setting-up exercises.
 2. Marching at quick or double time and running.
 3. Dumb-bell, club, and rifle exercises.
 4. Climbing.
 5. Jumping.
 6. Apparatus work.
 7. Gymnastic contests.
 8. Athletics.
 9. Swimming.
 10. Boxing and wrestling.

SCOPE. 7

Setting-up exercises are the foundation upon which the entire course of training in the service is based. Their importance can not be overestimated, as by means of them alone it is possible to effect an all-around development impossible of attainment by any other method. They should therefore form a very important part of every drill.

Marching in quick time and exercises calling into action the various parts of the body while marching tend to develop coordination, upon which to a great extent poise, posture, carriage, and rhythm are dependent. Marching in double time is a heart and lung developing exercise of moderate severity. Running, on the other hand, especially when continued for long periods, or at a high rate of speed, or when taken in conjunction with leg exercises, affects those organs in a very marked degree. Both double timing and running are invaluable in the development of endurance and organic vigor.

Dumb-bell exercises are closely allied to the setting-up exercises and differ from these only by the extra weight that is imposed by the bells, which should, however, never exceed 2 pounds.

Club exercises are of use principally as a means for the development of coordination and grace in the upper extremities; their weight, since muscular development is not aimed at, should not exceed 2 pounds.

Rifle exercises have for their object the development of "handiness" with the piece. Owing to the weight of the rifle they are powerful factors in the development of the muscles of the arms, upper back, shoulders, and chest, and when taken in conjunction with trunk and leg exercises they are excellent agents for the all-round development of those who possess the strength to wield the piece to advantage.

Climbing, on poles or ropes, when both arms and legs are used, brings into action nearly every muscle of the body and exerts considerable influence upon the heart. Where poles or ropes of sufficient length are used this exercise will also develop self-reliance.

Jumping, when indulged in as a gymnastic exercise, where a series of from 8 to 10 jumps of moderate length are executed successively, is essentially a leg and heart developing exercise. When form is insisted upon and the nature of the jump is varied by introducing various leg, arm, and trunk movements, it becomes a strong factor in the development of coordination.

Apparatus work should be supplementary to all other forms of training. The chief object of this work in the service should be to use it as a means for the development of the ability of the soldier to control his body while its weight is supported by or suspended from the arms and hands, in order to enable him to successfully overcome and surmount such obstacles as may present themselves during field service. The exercises composing this part of the training should, therefore, be confined to those that will develop the muscular strength of the entire body in general and that of the arms and legs in particular, and at the same time tend to make the soldier agile and active and teach him decision and self-reliance.

Gymnastic contests are the simpler forms of antagonistic gymnastics in which the participants are pitted against each other, and which never fail to induce the usual rivalry for superiority attending personal contests. Their chief value lies in the development of agility and quickness of thought and action. They are quite the most interesting of those exercises in which the effort is lost sight of in the desire to win.

Athletics, when employed for the sake of their value as a means for the development of large numbers, which should be the case in the service, have nothing in common with competitive athletics. In other words, their value lies entirely in their usefulness in the development of physical strength, endurance, and skill, and not in the making or breaking of records.

Swimming is of vital importance to everyone connected with the service, and it should be made obligatory upon all officers and enlisted men to make themselves proficient in it. Aside from its usefulness it is without doubt the best single means to all round physical development.

METHODS.

Boxing and *wrestling*, while not recommended as an obligatory part of the enlisted man's training, should still be encouraged at all times, not only on account of their value as a means to bodily development, but on account of the self-reliance and confidence they give to those who are proficient in them.

METHODS.

In the employment of the various forms of physical training enumerated above it is necessary that well-defined methods should be introduced in order that the object of this training may be attained in the most thorough and systematic manner. Whenever it is possible this work should be conducted out of doors. In planning these methods the following factors must be considered:

(a) The condition and physical aptitude of the men.
(b) The facilities.
(c) The time.
(d) Instruction material.

The question of the *physical aptitude* and *general condition*, etc., of the men is a very important one, and it should always determine the nature and extent of the task expected of them; never should the work be made the determining factor. In general, it is advisable to divide the men into three classes, viz, the recruit class, the intermediate class, and the advanced class. The work for each class should fit the capabilities of the members of that class and in every class it should be arranged progressively.

Facilities are necessarily to be considered in any plan of instruction, but as most posts are now equipped with better than average facilities the plan laid down in this Manual will answer all purposes.

Time is a decidedly important factor, and no plan can be made unless those in charge of this work know exactly how much time they have at their disposal. During the suspension of drills five periods a week, each of 45 minutes duration, should be devoted to physical training; during the drill period a 15-minute drill in setting-up exercises should be ordered on drill days. The time of day, too, is important. When possible, these drills should be held in the morning about two hours after breakfast, and at no time should they be held immediately before or after a meal.

The proper use of the *instruction material* is undoubtedly the most important part of an instructor's duty, for it not only means the selection of the proper material but its application. Every exercise has a function peculiarly its own; in other words, it has a certain effect upon a certain part of the body and plays a rôle in the development of the men. It is, therefore, the sum of these various exercises properly grouped that constitutes the method. So far as possible, every lesson should be planned to embrace setting-up exercises that call into action all parts of the body, applied gymnastics, apparatus work, and exercises that develop coordination and skill, such as jumping and vaulting.

The best results are obtained when these exercises which affect the extensor muscles chiefly are followed by those affecting the flexors; i. e., flexion should always be followed by extension, or vice versa. It is also advisable that a movement requiring a considerable amount of muscular exertion should be followed by one in which this exertion is reduced to a minimum. As a rule, especially in the setting-up exercises, one portion of the body should not be exercised successively; thus, arm exercises should be followed by a trunk exercise, and that in turn by a leg, shoulder, or neck exercise.

The following program of a week's work illustrates the application of the instruction material as described above: each drill is of 45 minutes duration:

First Day's Program.

1. Marching in quick and double time (5 minutes).
2. Setting-up exercises (15 minutes).
3. Applied gymnastics, flexor work, horizontal bar (15 minutes).
4. Jumping exercises (8 minutes).
5. Trunk and arm stretching exercises in conjunction with breathing exercises (2 minutes).

METHODS.

SECOND DAY'S PROGRAM.

1. Exercises in marching, combined with arm and leg exercises (10 minutes).
2. Setting-up exercises, chiefly trunk exercises (5 minutes).
3. Applied gymnastics, extensor work, parallel bars (15 minutes).
4. Vaulting, low vaulting bars (13 minutes).
5. Stretching and breathing exercises (2 minutes).

THIRD DAY'S PROGRAM.

1. Marching in double and quick time (5 minutes).
2. Setting-up exercises, general work (15 minutes).
3. Applied gymnastics, flexor work, rings (15 minutes).
4. Jumping exercises (8 minutes).
5. Stretching and breathing exercises (2 minutes).

FOURTH DAY'S PROGRAM.

1. Running and walking (5 minutes).
2. Setting-up exercises, general work (10 minutes).
3. Applied gymnastics, extensor work, side horse (15 minutes).
4. Climbing (13 minutes).
5. Stretching and breathing exercises (2 minutes).

FIFTH DAY'S PROGRAM.

1. Marching quick time, running, and exercises while marching in quick time (10 minutes).
2. Setting-up exercises, trunk movements (5 minutes).
3. Applied gymnastics, flexor work, horizontal bar (15 minutes).
4. Vaulting, side horse vaults (13 minutes).
5. Stretching and breathing exercises (2 minutes).

Clubs, dumb-bells, bar bells, wands, or rifles may be substituted for the setting-up exercises occasionally, and the gymnastic contests may also be used in place of the jumping and vaulting exercises.

Large numbers may be employed in a body in the setting-up exercises and also in the exercises with the clubs, etc. In the applied or apparatus work, unless the facilities afford a sufficient number of the same kind of apparatus, it is advisable to divide the men into small squads.

Officers who have been placed in charge of this work must not for an instant lose sight of the fact that to them has been intrusted a part of the soldier's training which is of great importance, and that success or failure is dependent entirely upon themselves. Work as important as this is worthy of the best efforts, and it should never be intrusted to those who are not enthusiastic about it.

Whenever possible the officer in charge should conduct the work personally, as in no profession does the individuality and personal influence of a leader carry such weight as it does in the military.

A well-defined program should be mapped out before the drill begins, and this should be carried out faithfully. Every day's work should dovetail into the next and be progressive.

Instructors should not fail to do as much as possible themselves, as an example is always more impressive than a precept; it will also serve to keep the officer in fit condition.

Where commands are large, the athletic officer should be given officer assistants, whom he should train so that they may be able to carry out his program intelligently. If officers are not available, he should select likely enlisted men and train them to be leaders capable of taking charge of a squad.

The work laid down in this manual should not be followed blindly; every instructor should select such portions, and if necessary vary them, as in his opinion are productive of the best results under the conditions under which he is laboring.

The work should be so conducted that the men are developed harmoniously; that is, any tendency to develop one side or one portion of the body at the expense of the other should be avoided.

Insist upon accurate and precise execution of every movement. By doing so those other essential qualities, besides strength and endurance—activity, agility, gracefulness, and accuracy—will also be developed.

Exercises which require activity and agility, rather than those that require strength only, should be selected.

It should be constantly borne in mind that these exercises are the means and not the end; and if there be a doubt in the mind of the instructor as to the effect of an exercise, it is always well to err upon the side of safety. *Underdoing is rectifiable; overdoing is often not.* The object of this work is not the development of expert gymnasts, but the development of physically sound men by means of a system in which the chances of bodily injury are reduced to a minimum. When individuals show a special aptitude for gymnastics they may be encouraged, within limits, to improve this ability, but never at the expense of their fellows.

The drill should be made attractive, and this can best be accomplished by employing the mind as well as the body. The movements should be as varied as possible, thus constantly offering the men something new to make them keep their minds on their work. A movement many times repeated presents no attraction and is executed in a purely mechanical manner which should always be discountenanced.

Short and frequent drills should be given in preference to long ones, which are liable to exhaust all concerned, and exhaustion means lack of interest and benefit. All movements should be carefully explained, and, if necessary, illustrated by the instructor.

The lesson should begin with the least violent exercises, gradually working up to those that are more so, then gradually working back to the simpler ones, so that the men at the close of the drill will be in as nearly a normal condition as possible.

When one portion of the body is being exercised, care should be taken that the other parts remain quiet so far as the conformation of the body will allow. The men must learn to exercise any one part of the body independent of the other parts.

Everything in connection with physical training should be such that the men look forward to it with pleasure, not with dread, for the mind exerts more influence over the human body than all the gymnastic paraphernalia that was ever invented.

Exercise should be carried on as much as possible in the open air; at all times in pure, dry air.

All the men except those excused by the post surgeon should be compelled to attend these drills.

Never exercise the men to the point of exhaustion. If there is evidence of panting, faintness, fatigue, or pain, the exercise should be stopped at once, for it is nature's way of saying "too much."

By constant practice the men should learn to breathe slowly through the nostrils during all exercises, especially while running.

A fundamental condition of exercise is unimpeded respiration. Proper breathing should always be insisted upon; "holding the breath" and breathing only when it can no longer be held is injurious. Every exercise should be accompanied by an unimpeded and if possible by an uninterrupted act of respiration, the inspiration and respiration of which depends to a great extent upon the nature of the exercise. Inhalation should always accompany that part of an exercise which tends to elevate and distend the thorax— as raising arms over head laterally, for instance; while that part of an exercise which exerts a pressure against the walls of the chest should be accompanied by exhalation, as for example, lowering arms laterally from shoulders or overhead.

If after exercising, the breathing becomes labored and distressed, it is an unmistakable sign that the work has been excessive. Such excessiveness is not infrequently the cause of serious injury to the heart and lungs, or to both. In cases where exercise produces palpitation, labored respiration, etc., it is advisable to recommend absolute rest, or to order such exercises that will relieve the oppressed and overtaxed organ. Leg exercises slowly executed will afford such relief; by drawing the blood from the upper to the lower extremities they equalize the circulation, thereby lessening the heart's action and quieting the respiration.

Never exercise immediately after a meal; digestion is more important at this time than extraneous exercise.

Never eat or drink immediately after exercise; allow the body to recover its normal condition first, and the most beneficial results will follow. If necessary, pure water, not too cold, may be taken in small quantities, but the exercise should be continued, especially if in a state of perspiration.

Never, if at all possible, allow the underclothing to dry on the body. Muscular action produces an unusual amount of bodily heat; this should be lost gradually, otherwise the body will be chilled; hence, after exercise, never remove clothing to cool off, but, on the contrary, wear some wrap in addition. In like manner, be well wrapped up on leaving the gymnasium.

Cold baths, especially when the body is heated, as in the case after exercising violently, should be discouraged. In individual instances such baths may appear apparently beneficial, or at least not injurious; in a majority of cases, however, they can not be used with impunity. Tepid baths are recommended. When impossible to bathe, the flannels worn while exercising should be stripped off, the body sponged with tepid water, and then rubbed thoroughly with coarse towels. After such a sponge the body should be clothed in clean, warm clothing.

Flannel is the best material to wear next to the body during physical drill, as it absorbs the perspiration, protects the body against drafts and in a mild manner excites the skin. When the conditions permit it the men may be exercised in the ordinary athletic costume, sleeveless shirt, flappers, socks, and gymnasium shoes.

COMMANDS—SETTING-UP EXERCISES.

COMMANDS.

There are two kinds of commands:

The preparatory indicates the movement to be executed.

The command of execution causes the execution.

In the command: 1. Arms forward, 2. RAISE, the words *Arms forward* constitute the preparatory command, and RAISE, the command of execution. Preparatory commands are printed in ordinary type, and those of execution in CAPITALS.

The tone of command is animated, distinct, and of a loudness proportioned to the number of men for whom it is intended.

The various movements comprising an exercise are executed by commands and, unless otherwise indicated, the continuation of an exercise is carried out by repeating the command, which usually takes the form of numerals, the numbers depending upon the number of movements that an exercise comprises. Thus, if an exercise consists of two movements, the counts will be one, two; or if it consists of eight movements, the counts will be correspondingly increased; thus every movement is designated by a separate command.

Occasionally, especially in exercises that are to be executed slowly, words rather than numerals are used, and these must be indicative of the nature of the various movements.

In the continuation of an exercise the preparatory command is explanatory, the command of execution causes the execution and the continuation is caused by a repetition of numerals denoting the number of movements required, or of words describing the movements if words are used. The numerals or words preceding the command HALT should always be given with a rising inflection on the first numeral or word of command of the last repetition of the exercise in order to prepare the men for the command HALT.

For example:

1. Arms to thrust, 2. RAISE, 3. Thrust arms upward, 4. EXERCISE, ONE, TWO, ONE, TWO, ONE, HALT; the rising inflection preparatory to the command HALT being placed on the "one" preceding the "HALT."

Each command must indicate, by its tone, how that particular movement is to be executed; thus, if an exercise consists of two movements, one of which is to be energized, the command corresponding to that movement must be emphasized.

Judgment must be used in giving commands, for rarely is the cadence of two movements alike; and a command should not only indicate the cadence of an exercise, but also the nature of its execution.

Thus, many of the arm exercises are short and snappy; hence the command should be given in a smart tone of voice, and the interval between the commands should be short.

The leg exercises can not be executed as quickly as those of the arms; therefore, the commands should be slightly drawn out and follow one another in slow succession.

The trunk exercises, owing to the deliberateness of execution, should be considerably drawn out and follow one another in slow succession.

The antagonistic exercises, where one group of muscles is made to antagonize another, tensing exercises, the commands are drawn still more. In these exercises words are preferable to numerals. In fact it should be the object of the instructor to convey to the men, by the manner of his command, exactly the nature of the exercise.

All commands should be given in a clear and distinct tone of voice, articulation should be distinct, and an effort should be made to cultivate a voice which will inspire the men with enthusiasm

SETTING-UP EXERCISES. 19

and tend to make them execute the exercises with willingness, snap, and precision. It is not the volume, but the quality, of the voice which is necessary to successful instruction.

Fig. A.

Fig. B.

THE POSITION OF ATTENTION.

This is the position an unarmed dismounted soldier assumes when in ranks. During the setting-up exercises, it is assumed whenever the command *attention* is given by the instructor.

Having allowed his men to rest, the instructor commands: 1. Squad, 2. ATTENTION. Figs. A and B.

The words *class*, *section*, or *company* may be substituted for the word "squad."

At the command attention, the men will quickly assume and retain the following position:

Heels on same line and as near each other as the conformation of the man permits.

Feet turned out equally and forming an angle of about 45 degrees.

Knees straight without stiffness.

The body erect on the hips, the spine extended throughout its entire length.

The shoulders falling naturally, are forced back until they are square.

Chest arched and slightly raised.

The arms hang naturally; thumbs along seams of trousers; back of hands out and elbows turned back.

Head erect, chin drawn in so that the axis of the head and neck is vertical; eyes straight to the front and, when the nature of the terrain permits it, fixed on an object at their own height.

Too much attention can not be given to this position, and instructors are cautioned to insist that the men accustom themselves to it. As a rule, it is so exaggerated that it not only becomes ridiculous, but positively harmful. The men must be taught to assume a natural and graceful position, one from which all rigidity is eliminated and from which action is possible without first relaxing muscles that have been constrained in an effort to maintain the position of attention. In other words, coordination rather than strength should be depended upon.

In the position described the weight rests principally upon the balls of the feet, the heels resting lightly upon the ground.

The knees are extended easily, but never locked.

The body is now inclined forward until the front of the thighs is directly over the base of the toes; the hips are square and the waist is extended by the erection of the entire spine, but never to such a degree that mobility of the waist is lost.

SETTING-UP EXERCISES. 21

In extending the spine, the chest is naturally arched and the abdomen is drawn in, but never to the extent where it interferes with respiration.

In extending the spinal column, the shoulders must not be raised, but held loosely in normal position and forced back until the points of the shoulders are at right angles with an anterior-posterior plane running through the body.

The chin should be square; i. e., horizontal and forced back enough to bring the neck in a vertical plane; the eyes fixed to the front and the object on which they are fixed must be at their own height whenever the nature of the terrain permits it.

When properly assumed, a vertical line drawn from the top of the head should pass in front of the ear, just in front of the shoulder and of the thigh, and find its base at the balls of the feet.

All muscles should be contracted only enough to maintain this position, which at all times should be a lithesome one, that can be maintained for a long period without fatigue—one that makes for activity and that is based upon a correct anatomical and physiological basis.

Instructors will correct the position of attention of every man individually and they will ascertain, when the position has been properly assumed, whether the men are "on their toes," i. e., carrying the weight on the balls of the feet, whether they are able to respire properly. This position should be repeated until the men are able to assume it correctly without restraint or rigidity.

At the command *rest* or *at ease* the men, while carrying out the provisions of the drill regulations, should be cautioned to avoid assuming any position that has a tendency to nullify the object of the position of attention; as standing on one leg for instance; allowing the shoulders to slope forward; drooping the head; folding arms across chest, etc. The weight should always be distributed equally upon both legs; the head, trunk, and shoulders remain erect and the

MANUAL OF PHYSICAL TRAINING.

arms held in a position that does not restrict the chest or derange the shoulders. The positions illustrated here have been found most efficacious. Figs. C and D.

FIG. C.

FIG. D.

FORMATIONS.

The men form in a single or double rank, the tallest men on the right.

The instructor commands: 1. Count off.

At this command, all except the right file execute "eyes right" and, beginning on the right, the men in each rank count 1, 2, 3, 4; each man turns his head and eyes to the front as he counts.

SETTING-UP EXERCISES.

The instructor then commands: 1. Take distance, 2. MARCH, 3. SQUAD, 4. HALT.

At the command march, No. 1 of the front rank moves straight to the front; Nos. 2, 3, and 4 of the front and Nos. 1, 2, 3, and 4 of the rear rank in the order named move straight to the front, each stepping off, so as to follow the preceding man at four paces; the command halt is given when all have their distances.

If it is desired that a less distance than four paces be taken, the distance desired should be indicated in the preparatory command. The men of the squad may be caused to cover No. 1 front rank by the command *cover*.

The instructor then commands: 1. Right (left), 2. FACE, 3. COVER.

At these commands the men face in the direction indicated and cover in file.

To assemble the squad the instructor commands: 1. Right (left), 2. FACE, 3. assemble, 4. MARCH.

After facing and at command march, No. 1 of the front rank stands fast, the other members of both ranks resuming their original positions, or for convenience in the gymnasium they may be assembled to the rear, in which case the assemblage is made on No. 4 of the rear rank.

Unless otherwise indicated, the guide is always right.

SPECIAL TRAINING.

In addition to the regular squad or class work instructors should, when they notice a physical defect in any man, recommend some exercise which will tend to correct it.

The most common physical defects and corresponding corrective exercises are noted here.

DROOPING HEAD.

Exercise the muscles of the neck by bending, turning, and circling the head, muscles tense.

ROUND AND STOOPED SHOULDERS.

Stretch arms sideward from front horizontal, turning palms upward, muscles tense.

Swing arms forward and backward, muscles relaxed.

Circle arms forward and backward slowly, energize backward motion, muscles tense; forward motion with muscles relaxed.

Circle shoulders backward, move them forward first, then raise them; then move them backward as far as possible in the raised position, muscles tense, and then lower to normal position, muscles relaxed.

Weak Back.

Bend trunk forward as far as possible and erect it slowly.

Bend trunk forward, back arched and head thrown back.

Bend trunk sideward, without moving hips out of normal position, right and left.

Lie on floor, face down, and raise head and shoulders.

Weak Abdomen.

Circle trunk right or left.

Bend trunk backward or obliquely backward.

Bend head and trunk backward without moving hips out of normal plane.

Lie on floor, face up, and raise head and shoulders slightly; or to sitting position or raise legs slightly; or to a vertical position.

To Increase Depth and Width of Chest.

Arm stretchings, sideward and upward, muscles tense.

Same, with deep inhalations.

Arm swings and arm circles outward, away from the body.

Raise extended arms over head laterally and cross them behind the head.

Breathing exercises in connection with arm and shoulder exercises.

SETTING-UP EXERCISES. 25

STARTING POSITIONS.

In nearly all the arm exercises it is necessary to hold the arms in some fixed position from which the exercise can be most advantageously executed, and to which position the arms are again returned

FIG. 1.

upon completing the exercise. These positions are termed *starting positions;* and though it may not be absolutely necessary to assume one of them before or during the employment of any other portion of the body, it is advisable to do so, since they give to the exercise a finished, uniform, and graceful appearance.

26 MANUAL OF PHYSICAL TRAINING.

In the following positions, at the command *down*, resume the *attention*. Practice in assuming the starting position may be had by repeating the commands of execution, such as *raise*, *down*.

Intervals having been taken and attention assumed, the instructor commands:

FIG. 2.

1. 1. Arms forward, 2. RAISE, 3. Arms, 4. DOWN. Fig. 1.

    At the command *raise*, raise the arms to the front smartly, extended to their full length, till the hands are in front of and at the height of the shoulders, palms down, fingers extended and joined, thumbs under index fingers. At ARMS, DOWN, resume position of attention.

2. 1. Arms sideward, 2. RAISE, 3. Arms, 4. DOWN. Fig. 2.

    At the command *raise*, raise the arms laterally until horizontal, palms down, fingers as in 1.

    The arms are brought down smartly without allowing them to touch the body.

SETTING-UP EXERCISES. 27

3. 1. Arms upward, 2. RAISE, 3. Arms, 4. DOWN. Fig. 3.

At the command *raise*, raise the arms from the sides, extended to their full length, with the forward movement, until they are vertically overhead, back of hands turned outward, fingers as in 1.

FIG. 3. FIG. 4.

This position may also be assumed by raising the arms laterally until vertical. The instructor cautions which way he desires it done.

4. 1. Arms backward, 2. CROSS, 3. Arms, 4. DOWN. Fig. 4.

At the command *cross*, the arms are folded across the back; hands grasping forearms.

28 MANUAL OF PHYSICAL TRAINING.

5. 1. Arms to thrust, 2. RAISE, 3. Arms, 4. DOWN. Fig. 5.

At the command *raise*, raise the forearms to the front until horizontal, elbow forced back, upper arms against the chest, hands tightly closed, knuckles down.

FIG. 5.   FIG. 6.

6. 1. Hands on hips, 2. PLACE, 3. Arms, 4. DOWN. Fig. 6.

At the command *place*, place the hands on the hips, the finger tips in line with trouser seams; fingers extended and joined, thumbs to the rear, elbows pressed back.

7. 1. Hands on shoulders, 2. PLACE, 3. Arms, 4. DOWN. Fig. 7.

At the command *place*, raise the forearms to the vertical positions, palms inward, without moving the upper arms; then raise the elbows upward and outward until the upper arms are horizontal; at the same time bending the wrist and allowing the finger tips to rest lightly on the shoulders.

SETTING-UP EXERCISES. 29

8. 1. Fingers in rear of head, 2. LACE, 3. Arms, 4. DOWN. Fig. 8.
At the command *lace*, raise the arms and forearms as described in 7, and lace the fingers behind the lower portion of the head, elbows well up and pressed well back.

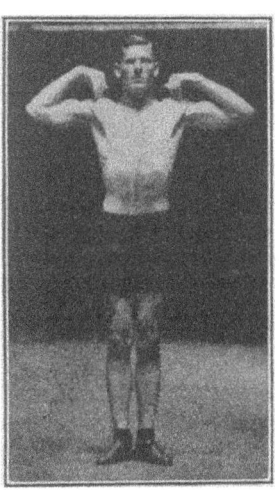 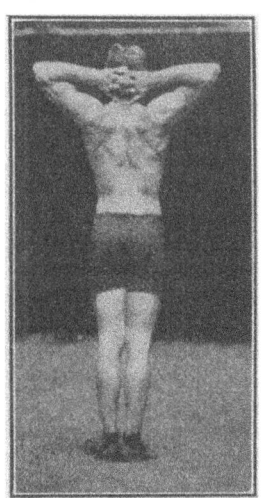

FIG. 7.   FIG. 8.

These positions should be practiced frequently, and instead of recovering the position of attention after each position, the instructor may change directly from one to another by giving the proper commands instead of commanding *arms, down*.

For instance: To change from the position described in paragraph 8 to that described in paragraph 9 (having commanded: 1. Hands on shoulders, 2. PLACE), he commands: 1. Hands on hips, 2. PLACE.

These changes should, however, be made only after the positions are thoroughly understood and correctly assumed.

SETTING-UP EXERCISES.

As has been stated previously (see par. 2), these exercises form the basis upon which the entire system of physical training in the service is founded. Therefore too much importance can not be attached to them. Through the number and variety of movements they offer it is possible to develop the body harmoniously with little if any danger of injurious results. They develop the muscles and impart vigor and tone to the vital organs and assist them in their functions; they develop endurance and are important factors in the development of smartness, grace, and precision. They should be assiduously practiced, and the fact that they require no apparatus of any description makes it possible to do this out of doors or even in the most restricted room, proper hygienic conditions being the only adjunct upon which their success is dependent. No physical training drill is complete without them. They should always precede the more strenuous forms of training, as they prepare the body for the greater exertion these forms demand.

The following series prescribed for the recruit and trained soldier's instruction is indicated here to illustrate the nature, amount, and arrangement of work that should be required of each class. At the discretion of instructors these exercises may be substituted by others of a similar character. Instructors are cautioned, however, to employ all the parts of the body in every lesson and to suit the exercise as far as practicable to the natural function of the particular part of the body which they employ.

In these lessons only the preparatory command is given here; the command of execution, which is invariably *Exercise*, and the commands of continuance, as well as the command to discontinue, having been explained in paragraph 6, are omitted.

Every preparatory command should convey a definite description of the exercise required; by doing so long explanations are avoided and the men will not be compelled to memorize the various movements.

SETTING-UP EXERCISES. 31

RECRUIT INSTRUCTION.
First Series.

1. Position of attention, from *at ease* and *rest*.
2. Starting positions, Par. 10, Figs. 1 to 8.
3. 1. Raise and lower arms to side horizontal.

    Two counts; repeat 8 to 10 times, Fig. 2.

    The arms rigidly extended are brought to the sides smartly without coming in contact with the thighs. Inhale on first and exhale on second count.

FIG. 9.

4. 1. Hands on hips, 2. PLACE, 3. Quarter bend trunk forward.

    Two counts; repeat 8 to 10 times, Fig. 9.

    The trunk is inclined forward at the waist about 45 degrees and then extended again; the hips are as perpendicular as possible; execute slowly; exhale on first and inhale and raise chest on second count.

5. 1. Arms to thrust, 2. RAISE, 3. Raise shoulders.

Two counts; repeat 8 to 10 times, Fig. 10.

The shoulders are raised as high as possible without deranging the position of the body or head and lowered back to position; execute briskly; inhale on first and exhale on second count.

FIG. 10.   FIG. 11.

6. 1. Hands on hips, 2. PLACE, 3. Quarter bend knees.

Two counts; repeat 8 to 10 times, Fig. 11.

The knees are flexed until the point of the knee is directly over the toes; whole foot remains on ground; heels closed; head and body erect; execute moderately fast, emphasizing the extension; breathe naturally.

SETTING-UP EXERCISES. 33

7. 1. Arms backward, 2. CROSS, 3. Rise on toes.

   Two counts; repeat 8 to 10 times, Fig. 12.

   The body is raised smartly until the toes and ankles are extended as much as possible; heels closed; head and trunk erect; in recovering position heels are lowered gently; breathe naturally.

FIG. 12.

8. 1. Breathing exercise, 2. INHALE, 3. EXHALE.

   At *inhale* the arms are stretched forward overhead and the lungs are inflated; at *exhale* the arms are lowered laterally and the lungs deflated; execute slowly; repeat four times.

MANUAL OF PHYSICAL TRAINING.

Second Series.

1. Position of attention, as in first series.
2. Repeat first lesson.
3. 1. Hands on shoulders, 2. PLACE, 3. Extend arms forward.
    Two counts; repeat 8 to 10 times.

    The arms are extended forward forcibly, palms down, and brought back to position smartly, elbows being forced back; exhale on first and inhale on second count.

Fig. 13.

4. 1. Hands on hips, 2. PLACE, 3. Bend trunk backward.
    Two counts; repeat 6 to 8 times, Fig. 13.

    The trunk is bent backward as far as possible; head and shoulders fixed; knees extended; feet firmly on the ground; hips as nearly perpendicular as possible; in recovering care should be taken not to sway forward; execute slowly; inhale on first and exhale on second count.

SETTING-UP EXERCISES.

5. 1. Arms to thrust, 2. RAISE, 3. Move shoulders forward.
    Two counts; repeat 8 to 10 times, Fig. 14.
    The shoulders are relaxed and moved forward and in as far as possible and then moved backward without jerking; head and trunk erect; execute slowly; exhale on first and inhale on second count.

FIG. 14.   FIG. 15.

6. 1. Arms backward, 2. CROSS, 3. Half bend knees.
    Two counts; repeat 8 to 10 times, Fig. 15.
    The knees are separated and bent halfway to the ground, point of knee being forced downward; head and trunk erect; execute smartly and emphasize the extension; breathe naturally.

36 MANUAL OF PHYSICAL TRAINING.

7. 1. Hands on hips, 2. PLACE, 3. Half bend trunk forward.
Two counts; repeat 8 to 10 times, Fig. 16.

The trunk is inclined forward until it is at right angles to the legs, hips perpendicular; knees extended; head and shoulders fixed; execute moderately slow; exhale on first and inhale and raise chest on second count.

FIG. 16.

8. 1. Hands on shoulders, 2. PLACE, 3. Strike arms sideward.
The arms, knuckles down, hands closed, are flung outward forcibly and brought back to shoulders smartly; execute fast; breathe naturally.
9. Breathing exercise, as in first lesson.

SETTING-UP EXERCISES.

Third Series.

1. Position of attention, as in first series.
2. Repeat second lesson.
3. 1. Raise arms overhead laterally.

    Two counts; repeat 8 to 10 times, as in Fig. 3.

    The arms, rigidly extended at the elbows, are raised overhead, palms inward, smartly and brought down the same way; execute moderately fast; inhale on the first and exhale on the second count.

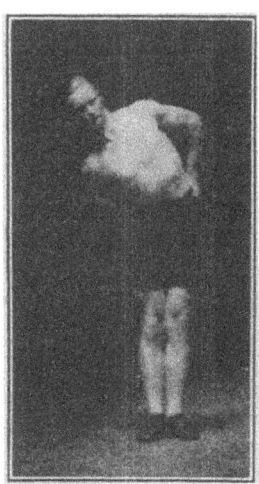

FIG. 17.

4. 1. Hands on hips, 2. PLACE, 3. Bend trunk sideward, right or left.

    Two counts; repeat 6 to 8 times, Fig. 17.

    The trunk, stretched at the waist, is inclined sideward as far as possible; head and shoulders fixed; knees extended and feet firmly on the ground; execute slowly; inhale on first and exhale on second count.

5. 1. Arms to thrust, 2. RAISE, 3. Bend head forward and backward.

Four counts; repeat 6 to 8 times, Fig. 18.

The chin is drawn in and the head bent forward, back muscles of neck being stretched upward; shoulders remain fixed; in recovering the muscles are relaxed; execute slowly; inhale and raise chest on first and exhale on second count. In bending the head backward the muscles of the neck are stretched upward; breathe as before.

FIG. 18.   FIG. 19.

6. 1. Curl shoulders forward.

Two counts; repeat 6 to 8 times, Fig. 19.

The shoulders relaxed are rolled forward as far as possible, arms being rotated forward; they are then rolled backward and the arms are rotated backward; execute slowly; exhale on first and inhale on second count.

SETTING-UP EXERCISES. 39

1. Hands on hips, 2. PLACE, 3. Full bend knees.

Two counts; repeat 6 to 8 times, Fig. 20.

The knees are separated and bent as much as possible; point of knees forced forward and downward; heels together; trunk and head erect; execute slowly; breathe naturally.

FIG. 20.

8. 1. Hands in rear of head, 2. LACE, 3. On toes, 4. RISE, 5. ROCK.

Two counts; repeat 6 to 8 times.

The body is raised on toes and then by short and quick; extensions and flections of the toes it is lowered and raised knees extended; heels together and free from the ground; breathe naturally.

9. Breathing exercise as in first lesson.

40   MANUAL OF PHYSICAL TRAINING.

Fourth Series.

1. Repeat third series.
2. 1. Arms to thrust, 2. RAISE, 3. Thrust arms forward.

    Two counts; repeat 8 to 10 times, Fig. 21.

    The arms, knuckles up, are thrust forward forcibly; in recovering the elbows are forced back; execute moderately fast; exhale on first and inhale on the second count.

FIG. 21.   FIG. 22.

3. 1. Hands on shoulders, 2. PLACE, 3. Twist trunk sideward, right or left.

    Two counts; repeat 6 to 8 times, Fig. 22.

    The trunk is turned to the right or left as far as possible; hips as nearly perpendicular as possible; shoulders square and head erect; knees extended and feet firm; execute slowly; inhale on first and exhale on second count.

SETTING-UP EXERCISES. 41

4. 1. Arms to thrust, 2. RAISE, 3. Turn head right, or left.
Two counts; repeat 6 to 10 times, Fig. 23.

The head, chin square, is turned to the right, or left, as far as possible, muscles of the neck being stretched; shoulders remain square; execute slowly; breathe naturally.

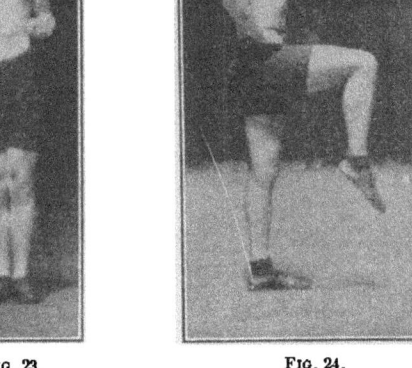

FIG. 23.　　　　　FIG. 24.

5. 1. Hands on hips, 2. PLACE, 3. Raise knee.
Two counts; repeat 10 to 12 times, Fig. 24.

The thigh and knee are flexed until they are at right angles, thigh horizontal; toes depressed; the right knee is raised at *one* and the left at *two;* trunk and head erect; execute in cadence of quick time; breathe naturally.

6. 1. Fingers in rear of head, 2. LACE, 3. Full bend trunk forward. FORWARD.

Two counts; repeat 6 to 8 times, Fig. 25.

The trunk is bent forward as far as possible; knees extended; feet firm; head and shoulders fixed; execute slowly; exhale on first and inhale on second count.

Fig. 25.

7. 1. Hands on hips, 2. PLACE, 3. On toes, 4. RISE, 5. HOP.

Two counts; repeat 12 to 16 times.

The body is raised on toes and the hopping is performed with knees extended; execute fast; breathe naturally.

8. Breathing exercise, as in first lesson.

SETTING-UP EXERCISES. 43.

Fifth Series.

1. Repeat fourth series.
2. 1. Arms forward, 2. RAISE, 3. Stretch arms sideward.
Two counts; repeat 6 to 8 times, Fig. 26.

FIG. 26.

From the front horizontal the arms are extended to their fullest extent and then stretched sideward, the arms rotating till the palms are up; the sideward movement is performed slowly; the recovery relaxed and quick; inhale on first and exhale on the second count.

MANUAL OF PHYSICAL TRAINING.

3. 1. Hands on hips, 2. PLACE, 3. Bend trunk obliquely forward, right or left.

   Two counts; repeat 4 to 8 times, Fig. 27.

   The trunk is turned to the right and bent forward to the half-bend position; shoulders remain square, in the plane of the ground; head fixed; knees straight; feet firm; hips as nearly perpendicular as possible; execute slowly; exhale on the first and inhale and raise chest on second count.

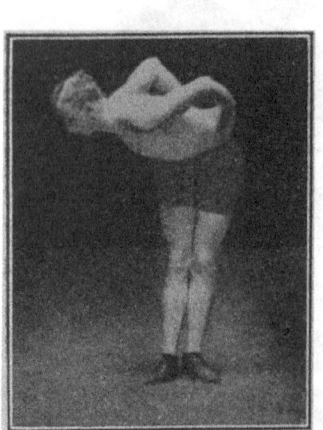 

FIG. 27. FIG. 28.

4. 1. Arms to thrust, 2. RAISE, 3. Extend leg forward.

   Two counts; repeat 8 to 10 times, Fig. 28.

   The knee and ankle are extended forward with a snap, the toes just escaping the ground; all extensor muscles contracted; in recovering relax; trunk and head erect; execute briskly; breathe naturally.

SETTING-UP EXERCISES. 45

5. 1. Hands on shoulders, 2. PLACE, 3. Move elbows forward.
    Two counts; repeat 8 to 10 times. Fig. 29.

    The elbows are brought together horizontally in front and then forced back as far as possible; the forward movement relaxed, the backward a stretch not a jerk; execute moderately fast; exhale on the first and inhale on the second count.

FIG. 29.

6. 1. Hand on hips, 2. PLACE, 3. Bend trunk forward and backward.

    Two counts; repeat 6 to 8 times.

    Bend trunk forward to the half-bend position (Fig. 16), and then backward (Fig. 13); execute slowly; exhale on first and inhale on second count.

7. 1. Arms backward, 2. CROSS, 3. Rise on toes, right and left alternately.

Four counts; repeat 10 to 12 times, Fig. 30.

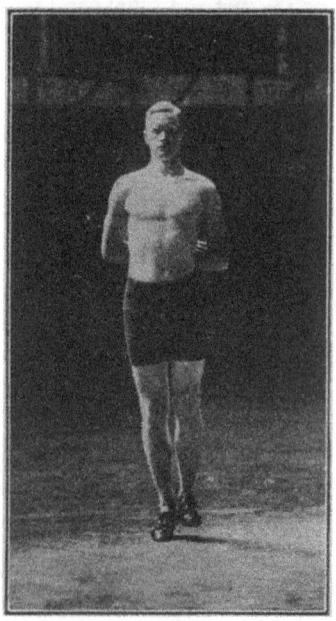

FIG. 30.

The body is extended on the toes of the right foot and then on those of the left; heels closed; trunk and head erect; execute moderately fast; breathe naturally.
8. Breathing exercise, as in first lesson.

SETTING-UP EXERCISES. 47

Sixth Series.

1. Repeat fifth series.
2. 1. Arms forward overhead, 2. RAISE, 3. Swing arms downward and upward.

    Two counts; repeat 8 to 10 times, Fig. 31.

FIG. 31.

3. 1. Arms sideward overhead, 2. RAISE, 3. Fingers, 4. LACE, 5. Bend trunk sideward, right and left.

    Two counts; repeat 6 to 8 times, Fig. 32.

    The arms are fully extended and the body, stretched at the waist, is bent sideward to the right and left; knees straight; feet firm; head erect; execute slowly; breathe naturally.

4. 1. Knees to squatting position, hands on hips, 2. BEND, 3. Rock on knees.

Two counts; repeat 6 to 8 times.

The knees are bent as in Fig. 20; extend and bend the knees in quick succession; trunk and head erect; heels closed; execute moderately fast; breathe naturally.

FIG. 32.

5. 1. Arms to thrust, 2. RAISE, 3. Move shoulders forward, up, back, and down.

Four counts; repeat 8 to 10 times.

The shoulders are relaxed and brought forward; in that position they are raised; then they are forced back without lowering them; and then they are dropped back to position; execute slowly; exhale on the first; inhale on the second and third and exhale on the last count.

SETTING-UP EXERCISES. 49

1. Arms to thrust, 2. RAISE, 3. Thrust arms forward; swing them sideward, forward, and back to position.

Four counts; repeat 8 to 10 times.

FIG. 33.

The arms are thrust forward, then relaxed and swung sideward, then forward and finally brought back to position, pressing elbows well to the rear; execute moderately fast; exhale on the first and third and inhale on the second and fourth counts.

50   MANUAL OF PHYSICAL TRAINING.

7. 1. Hop to side straddle and swing arms over head laterally and recover position of attention.

   Two counts; repeat 8 to 10 times, Fig. 33.

   The distance between the legs is about 30 inches; in alighting the toes come in contact with the ground first and knees are bent slightly; trunk and head erect; arms extended; execute moderately fast; breathe naturally.

8. Breathing exercise, as in first lesson.

FIG. 34.

TRAINED SOLDIERS' INSTRUCTION.

First Series.

1. 1. Stretch arms forward, sideward, forward and down.

   Four counts; repeat 6 to 8 times.

   The arms, stretched to their utmost, are raised forward horizontally, then moved sideward, knuckles down; in

SETTING-UP EXERCISES. 51

returning and lowering the arms the muscles are relaxed; trunk and head erect; execute first two motions slowly; second two moderately fast; inhale on first and second, and exhale on third and fourth counts.

2. 1. Hands on shoulders, 2. PLACE, 3. Half bend trunk forward and extend arms sideward.

Two counts; repeat 6 to 8 times, Fig. 34.

The trunk is bent as in Fig. 16, and arms are extended forcibly; in the recovery the elbows are forced back and the chest raised; execute slowly; exhale on first, inhale on second count.

FIG. 35.

3. 1. Hands on hips, 2. PLACE, 3. Full bend knees and extend arms sideward.

Two counts; repeat 6 to 8 times, Fig. 35.

The knees are bent as in Fig. 20, and arms are extended sideward forcibly; execute moderately slow; breathe naturally.

52   MANUAL OF PHYSICAL TRAINING.

4. 1. Arms sideward, 2. RAISE, 3. Roll shoulders and arms forward and back.

   Two counts; repeat 6 to 10 times, Fig. 36.

   The arms are rotated and the shoulders rolled forward and backward as far as possible; execute slowly; exhale on first and inhale and raise chest on second count.

FIG. 36.

5. 1. Hands on shoulders, 2. PLACE, 3. Twist trunk sideward right, or left, and extend arms sideward.

   Two counts; repeat 6 to 8 times, Fig. 37.

   The trunk is twisted as in Fig. 22; execute moderately fast; inhale on the first and exhale on the second count.

SETTING-UP EXERCISES. 53

6. 1. Raise arms and right or left leg forward, move arms sideward
and leg backward; move arms and leg forward and recover.

Four counts; repeat 8 to 10 times, Fig. 38.

On the first count, the arms and legs are raised forward,
arms horizontal, leg extended; toes depressed; foot at height

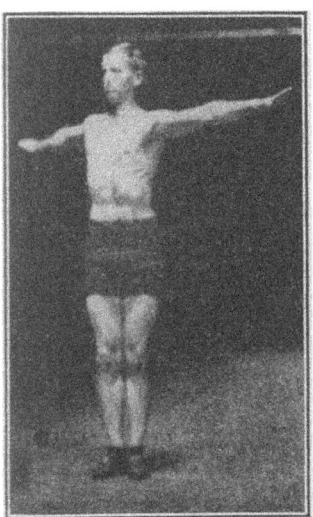 

FIG. 37.   FIG. 38.

of knee; on the second count the arms are moved smartly
to side horizontal and the leg is moved backward, knee and
toes extended; at *three* the first position is assumed and at *four*
the position of attention; execute moderately fast; inhale
on first two and exhale on last two counts.

54   MANUAL OF PHYSICAL TRAINING.

7. 1. Forearms vertically, 2. RAISE, 3. Extend arms upward and raise on toes; resume vertical position; and recover position of attention.

Four counts; repeat 8 to 10 times, Fig. 39.

FIG. 39.

The forearms are raised vertically at *one*; at *two* they are extended upward and the body is raised on toes; at *three* the first position is assumed, and at *four* the position of attention; execute briskly; inhale on first two and exhale on last two counts.

8. Breathing exercise.

SETTING-UP EXERCISES. 55

Second Series.
1. Repeat first series.
2. 1. Arms to thrust, 2. RAISE, 3. Thrust arms upward, swing downward and backward, swing upward and recover.

Four counts; repeat 6 to 10 times, Fig. 40.

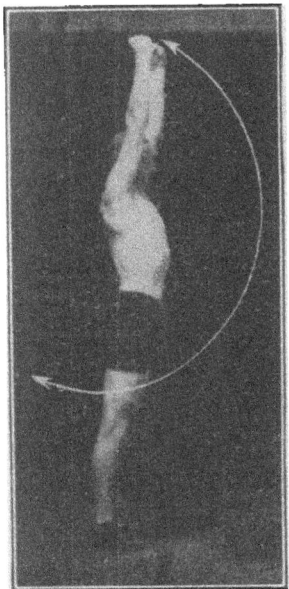
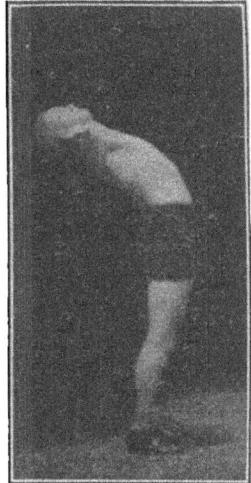

FIG. 40.　　　　FIG. 41.

The arms are thrust upward forcibly at *one*; at *two* the arms, relaxed, are swung downward to the front and back as far as possible; at *three* they are swung upward, and at *four* the position of attention is resumed; trunk and head erect; knees extended; execute moderately fast; inhale on first three and exhale on last count.

3. 1. Hands on shoulders, 2. PLACE, 3. Bend trunk backward and extend arms sideward, knuckles up.

Two counts; repeat 6 to 8 times, Fig. 41.

The trunk is bent backward as in Fig. 13, and the arms, knuckles down, are extended to the side horizontal; head fixed; knees extended; feet firm; execute slowly; inhale on first and exhale on second count.

FIG. 42.

4. 1. Full bend knees and raise arms, knuckles down, to side horizontal, 2. BEND, 3. Rock, and circle arms backward.

Two counts; repeat 6 to 10 times, Fig. 42.

The knees, bent to the squatting position, are slightly extended and flexed as in Exercise 4, Sixth Lesson, Recruit Instruction, and the arms are circled backward in circles of about 12 inches; head and trunk erect; arms extended; execute moderately fast; breathe naturally.

SETTING-UP EXERCISES. 57

5. 1. Hands on hips, 2. PLACE, 3. Circle trunk right, or left.

Six counts; repeat 4 to 6 times, Fig. 43.

The trunk is half bent forward at *one;* at *two* it is moved to the right side bend position; at *three* to the back bend; at *four* to the left bend; at *five* to the front bend position and raised at *six;* knees extended; feet firm; head fixed; execute slowly; exhale on first; inhale on second; hold breath on third and fourth; exhale on fifth and inhale on sixth count.

FIG. 43.

FIG. 44.

6. 1. Hands on hips, 2. PLACE, 3. Swing right and left leg forward, breast high, and extend right and left arm forward horizontally, alternating right and left.

Four counts; repeat 6 to 10 times, Fig. 44.

The right leg, knee extended, is swung forward high enough to come in contact with the hand; supporting leg extended; body inclined as little as possible; execute moderately fast; breathe naturally.

58 MANUAL OF PHYSICAL TRAINING.

7. 1. Leaning rest in four counts.

Repeat 6 to 8 times, Fig. 45 *a* and *b*.

At *one* knees are bent to squatting position, hands on the ground between knees; at *two* the legs are extended backward to the leaning rest; at *three* the first position is resumed,

FIG. 45 *a*. FIG. 45 *b*.

and at *four* the position of attention; hands should be directly under shoulders; back arched; knees straight; head fixed; execute moderately fast; breathe naturally.

8. Breathing exercise.

SETTING-UP EXERCISES. 59

Third Series.

1. Repeat second series.
2. 1. Stretch arms forward, sideward, upward, sideward, forward, and down.

    Six counts; repeat 6 to 10 times.

    First five counts arms are extended as much as possible; in the last they are relaxed; execute slowly; inhale on first three counts and exhale on last three.

FIG. 46.

3. 1. Half bend trunk forward and rotate arms inward; raise and bend trunk backward, raising and rotating arms backward, palms up; resume first position and recover.

    Four counts; repeat 4 to 8 times, Fig. 46.

    In the first position the body and arms are relaxed; in the second the body and arms are tense (Fig. 41); the third position is the same as the first, and at *four* the position of attention is resumed; execute slowly; exhale on first and third and inhale on second and fourth counts.

4. 1. Hands on hips, 2. PLACE, 3. Rise on toes, bend knees to squatting position; extend knees and recover.

Four counts; repeat 6 to 8 times.

The body is raised on toes slowly at *one;* at *two* the knees are bent slowly to squatting position; at *three* they are extended slowly and at *four* the starting position is resumed; execute slowly; breathe naturally.

FIG. 47.

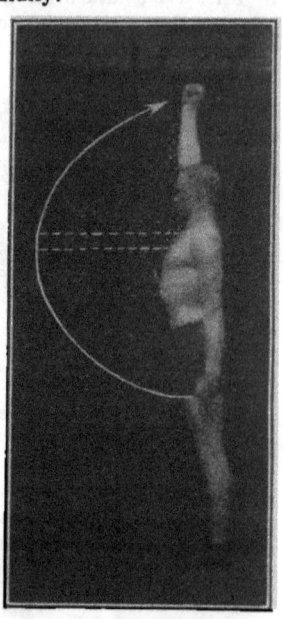

FIG. 48.

5. 1. Hop to side straddle position, hands on hips, bend trunk forward and extend arms downward, fingers touching ground; resume straddle with hands on hips and hop to attention.

Four counts; repeat 6 to 8 times, Fig. 47.

Execute moderately fast; breathe naturally.

SETTING-UP EXERCISES. 61

6. 1. Arms to thrust, 2. RAISE, 3. Thrust arms forward; swing right, (left) arm up, left, (right) down; swing to front horizontal and recover.

Four counts, or alternating in eight counts; repeat 8 to 10 times, Fig. 48.

The thrust and recovery are forcible, the swings brisk but relaxed; execute moderately fast; exhale on first and third count and inhale on second and fourth.

FIG. 49 a.   FIG. 49 b.

7. 1. Step position forward right, or left, and raise arms to front horizontal; lunge forward and swing arms to side horizontal; resume first position and recover position of attention.

Four counts; repeat 6 to 10 times, Fig. 49 a and b.

The right foot, knee extended and toes depressed, is moved forward once its length, the toes resting on the ground lightly, the weight resting on the left leg, and the arms are raised to the front horizontal, at *one;* at *two* the right foot is advanced and planted smartly, the distance between heels being about 3-foot lengths, and the arms are swung to side horizontal; right knee is well bent, left extended; trunk and head erect; at *three* the first position, and at *four* the position of attention are resumed; execute moderately fast; exhale on first and and third and inhale on second and fourth counts.

8. Breathing exercise.

FIG. 50.

Fourth Series.

1. Repeat third series.
2. 1. Hands on shoulders, 2. PLACE, 3. Extend arms upward, swing arms downward laterally, upward laterally, and recover starting position.

   Four counts; repeat 6 to 10 times.

SETTING-UP EXERCISES.

The first and fourth motions are energetic; the second and third relaxed; execute moderately fast; inhale on first and third counts and exhale on second and fourth.

3. 1. To side straddle with arms overhead, 2. Hop, 3. Bend trunk forward and back and swing arms downward and upward.

Two counts; repeat 6 to 8 times, Fig. 50.

FIG. 51.

Being in the straddle position, the body is bent forward as far as possible and the arms are swung between the legs; the arms are then swung upward and the body bent backward; knees extended; execute moderately fast; exhale on first and inhale on second count.

64 **MANUAL OF PHYSICAL TRAINING.**

4. 1. Arms to thrust, 2. RAISE, 3. Thrust arms sideward and lunge sideward right and left alternately.

Four counts; repeat 8 to 10 times, Fig. 51.

Fig. 52.

The starting position is resumed at *two* and *four;* the distance of the lunge is three times the length of the feet; supporting leg extended; head and trunk erect; execute moderately fast; inhale on first and third and exhale on second and fourth counts.

SETTING-UP EXERCISES. 65

5. 1. Hands on shoulders, 2. PLACE, 3. Bend trunk sideward right and extend left arm obliquely upward and right obliquely downward; swing trunk sideward left and right and recover.

Four counts; repeat 6 to 8 times, Fig. 52.

The trunk is bent to the right, the left arm, palm down, is extended obliquely upward and the right arm obliquely downward, at *one;* at *two* the body is bent to the left; at *three* to the right and at *four* the starting position is resumed; arms extended; knees straight; head fixed; execute moderately fast; breathe naturally.

FIG. 53.

6. 1. To squatting position, hands on ground. 2. BEND. 3. Extend right and left legs backward, alternately.

Four counts; repeat 6 to 10 times, Fig. 53.

The squatting position is the starting position, from there the right and left legs are extended backward and brought back to the squatting position again; execute moderately fast; breathe naturally.

66 MANUAL OF PHYSICAL TRAINING.

7. 1. Hands on shoulders. 2. PLACE, 3. Extend arms sideward and swing right and left legs sideward, alternately
Four counts; repeat 8 to 10 times, Fig. 54.

Fig. 54.

The legs are extended and swung loosely to the side as high as possible, arms being extended with each leg movement; execute moderately fast; inhale on *one* and *three* and exhale on *two* and *four*.

8. Breathing exercise.

SETTING-UP EXERCISES.

Fifth Series.

This series is composed of three groups, each group containing four exercises, and together they form a combination which can be adapted to music.

Each exercise is composed of four movements and should be repeated four times, twice to the right and twice to the left, alternately, except the last, which is repeated in the same direction. The third position always corresponds to the first, and the fourth to the position of attention.

When performed to music it is advisable to employ "two-four" time, allowing two beats to every movement, or four measures to an exercise, the action occurring on the first beat and a pause in position during the second beat. If this is done and the tempo is made to suit the movements, it will be possible to execute the exercises with precision and vigor, and slurring a movement for the sake of keeping time will be eliminated. Every group should be preceded by an introduction of four measures.

68 MANUAL OF PHYSICAL TRAINING.

First Group.

First Exercise.

Fig. 55.   Fig. 56.

Counts.
1—2. Raise arms overhead laterally and step position forward right. Fig. 55.
3—4. Lunge forward right and swing the arms downward and backward laterally. Fig. 56.
5—6. Resume first position.
7—8. Resume position of attention.
    Repeat left, right, left.

Second Exercise.

FIG. 57.   FIG. 58.

Counts.
1—2. Raise right arm obliquely upward to the right, and left arm obliquely backward to the left, and step position forward to the right with the right foot.   Fig. 57.
3—4. Lunge obliquely forward to the right and swing right arm downward to the rear, and left arm obliquely upward, Fig. 58.
5—6. Resume first position.
7—8. Resume position of attention.
Repeat left, right, left.

70   MANUAL OF PHYSICAL TRAINING.

Third Exercise.

FIG. 59.   FIG. 60.

Counts.
1—2. Flex arms over shoulders with lateral motion, knuckles to the
    rear, hands closed, and step position sideward right.   Fig. 59.
3—4. Lunge sideward right and extend arms to side horizontal,
    knuckles to the rear.   Fig. 60.
5—6. Resume first position.
7—8. Resume position of attention.
    Repeat left, right, left.

SETTING-UP EXERCISES. 71

Fourth Exercise.

FIG. 61. FIG. 62.

Counts.
1—2. Raise arms to side horizontal and step position backward right. Fig. 61.
3—4. Lunge backward right and raise arms overhead, knuckles out. Fig. 62.
5—6. Resume first position.
7—8. Resume position of attention.
   Repeat left, right, left.

SECOND GROUP.
First Exercise.

FIG. 63.

Counts.
1—2. Lunge forward right and raise arms to side horizontal. Fig. 63.
3—4. Bend trunk forward and move arms downward. Fig. 64.
5—6. Resume first position.
7—8. Resume position of attention.
 Repeat left, right, left.

SETTING-UP EXERCISES. 73

FIG. 64.

MANUAL OF PHYSICAL TRAINING.

Second Exercise.

FIG. 65.

Counts.
1—2. Lunge sideward right and raise right arm obliquely upward, and left arm obliquely downward. Fig. 65.
3—4. Bend trunk sideward right and swing left arm upward, knuckles out, and right arm downward in rear of body, knuckles out. Fig. 66.
5—6. Resume first position.
7—8. Resume position of attention.
  Repeat left, right, left.

Fig. 66.

76   MANUAL OF PHYSICAL TRAINING.

Third Exercise.

FIG. 67.

Counts.
1—2. Lunge obliquely forward to the right, and raise arms overhead laterally. Fig. 67.
3—4. Bend trunk forward and swing arms downward and upward. Fig. 68.
5—6. Resume first position.
7—8. Resume position of attention.
   Repeat left, right, left.

SETTING-UP EXERCISES. 77

Fig. 68.

78 MANUAL OF PHYSICAL TRAINING.

Fourth Exercise.

FIG. 69.

Counts.
1—2. Lunge backward right and raise arms to side horizontal, knuckles up. Fig. 69.
3—4. Bend trunk and head backward and raise arms overhead palms in. Fig. 70.
5—6. Resume first position.
7—8. Resume position of attention.
    Repeat left, right, left.

Fig. 70.

Third Group.

First Exercise.

Fig. 71.

Counts.
1—2. Stride forward right and flex arms over shoulders laterally, hands closed, knuckles up. Fig. 71.
3—4. Face to the left on both heels, bending knees and striking arms sideward, knuckles down. Fig. 72.
5—6. Resume first position.
7—8. Resume position of attention.
  Repeat left, right, left.

SETTING-UP EXERCISES.

Fig. 72.

82　MANUAL OF PHYSICAL TRAINING.

Second Exercise.

FIG. 73.

Counts.
1—2. Stride sideward right and raise and circle arms outward, crossing them below. Fig. 73.
3—4. Bend right knee and trunk obliquely forward, clasp thigh with arms. Fig. 74.
5—6. Resume first position.
7—8. Resume position of attention.
　　Repeat left, right, left.

SETTING-UP EXERCISES.

FIG. 74.

84 MANUAL OF PHYSICAL TRAINING.

Third Exercise.

FIG. 75.   FIG. 76.

Counts.
1—2. Stride backward right, and raise arms overhead laterally, palms in. Fig. 75.
3—4. Turn about on both heels, bend left knee and trunk backward and lower arms to side horizontal, palms up. Fig. 76.
5—6. Resume first position.
7—8. Resume position of attention.
   Repeat left, right, left.

SETTING-UP EXERCISES.

Fourth Exercise.

FIG. 77.

Counts.
1—2. Bend to the squatting position, hands on the ground. Same as Fig. 45a.
3—4. Extend to the leaning-rest with legs straddled. Fig. 77.
5—6. Resume first position.
7—8. Resume position of attention.
  Repeat four times.

NOTE.—Length of stride in these exercises should be 28 inches between heels.

HOPPING EXERCISES.

Hopping is executed by raising the body on the balls of the feet and forcing the body from the ground by a series of quick extensions of the toe and ankle joints; knees remain easily extended, heels together and free from the floor.

Having assumed a position for the arms, the instructor commands: 1. On toes. 2. RISE. 3. HOP.

At the command *hop*, execute one spring, alighting on the balls of the feet. Continue by repeating *one, two*.

1. Hop and turn to the right or left at every second, fourth, or sixth hop.
2. Hop and turn about at every second, fourth, or sixth hop.
3. Hop to side straddle in four and return to attention in four hops.
4. Hop to side straddle and continue to hop in that position.
5. Hop to side straddle in one hop and return to attention in next hop.
6. Hop to cross straddle and return to attention in next hop.
7. Hop on right leg and extend leg left forward, sideward, or backward.
8. Hop on left leg and extend right forward, sideward, or backward.
9. Hop four times on right leg, and then change and hop four times on left leg, extending the unemployed leg forward, sideward, or backward.
10. Same as in 9, hopping twice on each leg.
11. Same as in 9, hopping once on each leg.
12. Hop forward, sideward, or backward.

LEAPING.

Leaping or jumping as a setting-up exercise has for its object the raising of the body from 8 to 12 inches from the ground, there is, however, no gaining of ground as in gymnastic or athletic jumping.

At the first command, the arms are raised to the front horizontal and the body is elevated on the toes. (*See* Fig. 1, Jumping.)

SETTING-UP EXERCISES.

At the command *leap*, the arms are swung downward and backward and the knees are slightly bent (*see* Fig. 2, Jumping); without pausing the arms are swung forward again and as they pass through the vertical plane the knees are extended and the body is forced from the floor.

The moment the feet leave the floor the knees are extended; feet are closed and toes depressed; the arms are in the front horizontal; the back is arched and the head is erect. (*See* Fig. 3, Jumping.)

In alighting, the balls of the feet touch the floor first, knees slightly bent; the latter are quickly extended, however, and the arms brought down by the sides and the position of attention is assumed.

Continue by repeating *leap*.

LEAPING EXERCISES.

1. Leap and execute a quarter turn to the right or left.
2. Leap and execute a half turn to the right or left.
3. Leap and straddle legs sideward (legs are closed) before alighting.
4. Leap and cross straddle, right or left leg forward.
5. Leap and cross legs, right over left or left over right.
6. Leap and raise heels.
7. Leap and raise knees.
8. Leap and strike feet together.
9. Leap and strike feet together twice.
10. Leap and strike feet together three times.
11. Leap and cross and recross legs.
12. Leap and raise heels and touch them with hands.
13. Leap and swing arms sideward.
14. Leap and swing arms upward.
15. Leap and circle arms forward.
16. Leap and circle arms backward.
17. Leap and circle arms inward.
18. Leap and circle arms outward.
19. Leap and swing arms upward and execute a whole turn.

WALKING AND MARCHING.

The length of the full step in quick time is 30 inches, measured from heel to heel, and the cadence is at the rate of 120 steps per minute.

Proper posture and carriage have ever been considered very important in the training of soldiers. In marching, the head and trunk should remain immobile, but without stiffness; as the left foot is carried forward the right forearm is swung forward and inward obliquely across the body until the thumb, knuckles being turned out, reaches a point about the height of the belt plate. The upper arm does not move beyond the perpendicular plane while the forearm is swung forward, though the arm hangs loosely from the shoulder joint. The forearm swing ends precisely at the moment the left heel strikes the ground; the arm is then relaxed and allowed to swing down and backward by its own weight until it reaches a point where the thumb is about the breadth of a hand to the rear of the buttocks. As the right arm swings back, the left arm is swung forward with the right leg. The forward motion of the arm assists the body in marching by throwing the weight forward and inward upon the opposite foot as it is planted. The head is held erect; body well stretched from the waist; chest arched, and there should be no rotary motion of the body about the spine.

As the leg is thrown forward the knee is smartly extended, the heel striking the ground first.

The instructor having explained the principles and illustrated the step and arm swing, commands: 1. Forward, 2. MARCH—and to halt the squad he commands: 1. Squad, 2. HALT.

In executing the setting-up exercises on the march the cadence should at first be given slowly and gradually increased as the men become more expert; as some exercises require a slow and others a faster pace, it is best in these cases to allow the cadence of the exercise to determine the cadence of the step.

SETTING-UP EXERCISES.

The men should march in a single file at proved intervals. The command that causes and discontinues the execution should be given as the left foot strikes the ground.

On the march, to discontinue the exercise, command: 1. Quick time, 2. MARCH, instead of HALT, as when standing.

All of the arm, wrist, finger, and shoulder exercises, and some of the trunk and neck, may be executed on the march by the same commands and in the same manner as when standing.

The following leg and foot exercises are executed at the command *march;* the execution always beginning with the left leg or foot.

1. 1. On toes, 2. MARCH.
2. 1. On heels, 2. MARCH.
3. 1. On right heel and left toe, 2. MARCH.
4. 1. On left heel and right toe, 2. MARCH.
5. 1. On toes with knees extended, 2. MARCH.
6. 1. Swing extended leg forward, ankle high, 2. MARCH.
7. 1. Swing extended leg forward, knee high, 2. MARCH.
8. 1. Swing extended leg forward, waist high, 2. MARCH.
9. 1. Swing extended leg forward, shoulder high, 2. **MARCH.**
10. 1. Raise heels, 2. MARCH.
11. 1. Raise knees, thigh horizontal, 2. MARCH.
12. 1. Raise knees, chest high, 2. MARCH.
13. 1. Circle extended leg forward, ankle high, 2. **MARCH.**
14. 1. Circle extended leg forward, knee high, 2. **MARCH.**
15. 1. Circle extended leg forward, waist high, 2. **MARCH.**
16. 1. Swing extended leg backward, 2. MARCH.
17. 1. Swing extended leg sideward, 2. MARCH.
18. 1. Raise knee and extend leg forward, 2. **MARCH.**
19. 1. Raise heels and extend leg forward, 2. **MARCH.**

STEPS.

In the steps, the rules given above apply, viz, **the command** march given as the left foot strikes the ground, **determines the execution,** which always begins with the left foot, **and is continued until the** command: 1. Quick time, 2. MARCH, is given, when the direct step is resumed.

The different steps are executed at the following commands:

1. Cross step, 2. MARCH.

> As the legs move forward they are crossed. The body does not turn.

1. Halting step, 2. MARCH.

> The left foot is advanced and planted; the right foot is brought directly in rear of the left, resting on the ball only; the right is then advanced and planted and the left brought up, and so on.

1. Foot-balancing step, 2. MARCH.

> The left foot is advanced and planted; the right foot is brought up beside it, heels touching; the body is then raised on the toes and lowered. The right foot is then advanced and planted and the left brought up, and so on.

1. Continuous change step, 2. MARCH.

> The left foot is advanced and planted; the toes of the right are then advanced near the heel of the left in the halting step; the left foot is then advanced about half a step (15 inches) and the right foot is advanced with the full step and planted; the toes of the left foot are then brought up to the heel of the right foot, which advances a half step, when the left foot is advanced a full step, and so on.

1. Knee-rocking step, 2. MARCH.

> As each foot is planted it is accompanied by a slight bending and extension in the corresponding knee; the other leg remaining fully extended, heel raised.

1. Lunging step, 2. MARCH.

> The length of the step is 45 inches, the knee in advance being well bent; the other leg remaining fully extended, heel raised; trunk erect.

SETTING-UP EXERCISES. 91

1. Leg-balance step, 2. MARCH.

The left foot is advanced, ankle high; it is then swung backward and forward and planted, the body during the swing balancing on the right leg. The right foot is then advanced, swung backward and forward and planted, and so on.

1. Body-balance step, 2. MARCH.

The left foot is advanced, ankle high, body being bent slightly to the rear; the left foot is then swung backward, body being bent slightly to the front; the same foot is then swung forward again and planted, the body in the meantime becoming erect. This is repeated with the right foot, and so on.

1. Heel-and-toe step, 2. MARCH.

The left foot is advanced and allowed to rest on the heel; it is then swung backward and allowed to rest on the toes; it is once more advanced and planted. This is repeated with the right foot, and so on.

1. Cross step, raising knees, 2. MARCH.

Execute the cross step and raise the knees. The cross step may also be executed in combination with the swings of the extended leg.

The change step may be combined with the following: Cross step, halting step, raising knees, foot-rocking step, on toes, raising heels, swinging and circling legs, heel and toe step. These may also be combined with the change step hop.

1. Continuous change step hop, 2. MARCH.

Execute the ordinary change step, hopping with the change.

1. Forward gallop hop, 2. MARCH.

The left foot is advanced and planted, the right is brought up in rear as in the halting step; this is done four times in succession. The same is done four times with the right foot in advance, and so on.

1. Sideward gallop hop, 2. MARCH.

The left foot is advanced, body turning on the right; four hops are then executed sideward on the left foot followed by the right; at the fourth hop the body is turned to the left about and four hops executed sideward on the right foot followed by the left, and so on.

DOUBLE TIMING.

The length of the step in double time is 36 inches; the cadence is at the rate of 180 steps per minute. To march in double time the instructor commands: 1. Double time, 2. MARCH.

If at a halt, at the first command shift the weight of the body to the right leg. At the command March raise the forearms, fingers closed, to a horizontal position along the waist line; take up an easy run with the step and cadence of double time, allowing a natural swinging motion to the arms inward and upward in the direction of the opposite shoulder.

In marching in quick time, at the command, double time, *march*, given as either foot strikes the ground, take one step in quick time, and then step off in double time.

When marching in double time and in running the men breathe as much as possible through the nostrils, keeping the mouth closed.

A few minutes at the beginning of the setting-up exercises should be devoted to double timing. From lasting only a few minutes at the start it may be gradually increased, so that daily drills should enable the men at the end of five or six months to double time for 10 or 15 minutes without becoming fatigued or distressed.

After the double time the men should be marched for several minutes at quick time; after this the instructor should command:
1. Route step, 2. MARCH.

> In marching at route step, the men are not required to preserve silence nor keep the step; if marching at proved intervals, the latter is preserved.
>
> To resume the cadence step in quick time, the instructor commands: 1. Squad, 2. ATTENTION.

SETTING-UP EXERCISES.

Great care must be exercised concerning the duration of the double time and the speed and duration of the run. The demands made upon the men should be increased gradually.

When exercise rather than distance is desired, the running should be done on the balls of the feet, heels raised from the ground.

DOUBLE-TIMING EXERCISES.

While the men are double timing the instructor may vary the position of the arms by commanding:

1. 1. Arms forward, 2. RAISE.
2. 1. Arms sideward, 2. RAISE.
3. 1. Arms upward, 2. RAISE.
4. 1. Hands on hips, 2. PLACE.
5. 1. Hands on shoulders, 2. PLACE.
6. 1. Arms forward, 2. CROSS.
7. 1. Arms backward, 2. CROSS.

At the command *Arms, Down,* the double-time position for the arms and hands is resumed.

The instructor may combine the following with the double time:

1. 1. Cross step, 2. MARCH.
2. 1. Raise knees, 2. MARCH.
3. 1. Raise heels, 2. MARCH.
4. 1. Swing legs forward, 2. MARCH.
5. 1. Swings legs backward, 2. MARCH.

To continue these exercises, but still continue the double timing, command: 1. Double time, 2. MARCH. To march in quick time, command: 1. Quick time, 2. MARCH. Marching in quick or double time, to halt, command: 1. Squad, 2. HALT.

DUMB-BELLS.

These exercises are similar in every way to the setting-up exercises, in fact all of the latter may be performed with the dumb-bells. The object of these exercises is, therefore, the same as that of the setting-up exercises, except that the weight of the dumb-bells necessitates a greater expenditure of muscular energy, chiefly on the part of the muscles of the arms, shoulders, and upper back and chest.

It is advisable that light, wooden dumb-bells weighing from 2 to 2½ pounds be used, as the amount of additional exertion this weight calls for is sufficient for the purpose of muscular development without detracting from the activity and suppleness with which an exercise may be performed.

Dumb-bell exercises should be restricted to those who have been thoroughly drilled in the setting-up exercises.

For the sake of uniformity the dumb-bells will, unless otherwise specified, be held as follows: In all positions in which the arms assume a horizontal position the dumb-bells are vertical, and when the arms are in a vertical plane the plane of the bells is horizontal. The grip on the bells should, as a rule, always be firm.

The following is a series of dumb-bell exercises arranged progressively in lessons in order to illustrate the method of instruction for the benefit of instructors. The numerals in brackets are the counts on which that part of an exercise that precedes them is performed.

Whenever the word "recover" is used it signifies a return to the starting position.

MANUAL OF PHYSICAL TRAINING.

First Series.

Attention; at this command, the position of attention is assumed with bells hanging by the sides of the body, knuckles out.

Fig. 1.

From front horizontal position.

1. Swing bells downward (1) and forward (2).
2. Swing bells sideward (1) and forward (2).

From bells to thrust position.

3. Half bend trunk forward and thrust bells downward (1) Fig. 1; recover starting position (2).

DUMB-BELLS.

From attention.

4. Half bend knees and raise bells to side horizontal (1); recover (2).

FIG. 2.

From bells to thrust position.

5. Thrust bells upward and bend trunk backward (1) Fig. 2; recover (2).

From attention.

6. Rise on toes and raise bells overhead forward (1); recover (2).

98 MANUAL OF PHYSICAL TRAINING.

From front horizontal.

7. Bend trunk sideward and move bells sideward (1) Fig. 3, recover (2). Alternate right and left.

FIG. 3.

From attention.

8. Swing bells upward (1) and downward to the rear (2).

DUMB-BELLS.

Second Series.

From right bell extended overhead.

1. Swing right bell downward and left upward (1); left downward and right upward (2).

Fig. 4.

From bells on shoulders.

2. Strike bells sideward, knuckles down, and full bend knees (1) Fig. 4; recover (2).

From front horizontal.

3. Swing bells downward and backward and half bend trunk forward (1) Fig. 5; recover (2).

FIG. 5.

From attention.

4. Swing bells over head forward and raise right leg backward (1); recover (2); repeat with left leg, or alternate legs, and count four.

DUMB-BELLS. 101

From thrust position.

5. Thrust left bell upward, right downward, and bend trunk sideward right (1); recover (2); repeat to the left, or alternate, and count four.

FIG. 6.

6. Thrust bells sideward and lunge forward right (1) Fig. 6; recover (2); repeat to the left, or alternate.

102   MANUAL OF PHYSICAL TRAINING.

From bells on hips.

7. Extend bells sideward and bend trunk backward (1) Fig. 7; recover (2).

FIG. 7.

From attention.

8. Swing bells overhead and down laterally; upward (1); downward (2).

DUMB-BELLS. 103

THIRD SERIES.

From thrust position.

1. Thrust bells forward (1); swing sideward (2); swing forward (3); and recover (4).

FIG. 8.

From front horizontal.

2. Swing bells downward and bend trunk forward (1); swing bells forward and upward and bend trunk backward (2). Continuous motion.

From attention.

3. Raise bells to side horizontal and raise right leg sideward (1); recover (2); repeat left, or alternate in four counts.

Fig. 9.

From thrust position.

4. Twist trunk to the right and thrust bells sideward (1), Fig. 8; recover (2); repeat to the left, or alternate in four counts.
5. Thrust bells sideward and full bend knees (1); recover (2).

DUMB-BELLS. 105

From side straddle position, bells in side horizontal.

6. Bend trunk sideward right (1); and left (2); or in four counts.

FIG. 10.

From attention.

7. Swing bells overhead laterally and lunge sideward right (1), Fig. 9; recover (2); repeat left, or alternate in four counts.

From attention.

8. Raise bells to side horizontal and hop to side straddle (1), Fig. 10; recover (2).

Fourth Series.

From attention.

1. Stretch bells forward (1); stretch sideward (2); stretch forward (3); recover (4).

From attention.

2. Raise bells to front horizontal and step position forward right (1); lunge forward right and move arms to side horizontal (2); third position same as the first (3); recover (4); repeat left, or alternate right and left in eight counts.

From side straddle, bells to thrust.

3. Bend trunk forward and thrust bells to the floor (1); recover (2); bend trunk backward and thrust bells sideward (3); recover (4).

From front horizontal.

4. Twist trunk to the right and swing arms sideward (1); recover (2); repeat to the left, or alternate in four counts.

From attention.

5. Bend knees to the squatting position and place bells on the floor between the feet (1); extend legs backward to leaning rest (2); recover squatting position (3); recover attention (4).

From front horizontal.

6. Move bells sideward, turning thumbs down, and half bend knees (1), Fig. 11; raise bells overhead and extend knees (2); resume side horizontal with knees bent (3); recover (4).

DUMB-BELLS.

FIG. 11.

From bells on hips.

7. Lunge obliquely forward right and place bells on either side of feet (1); recover (2); repeat to the left, or alternate.

Fig. 12.

From side straddle, bells overhead.

8. Twist trunk to the right and lower bells to side horizontal (1) Fig. 12; raise bells and twist trunk forward (2); repeat to the left, or alternate in four counts.

DUMB-BELLS.

Fifth Series.
From attention.

1. Stretch bells to side horizontal (1); stretch overhead and rise on toes (2); lower to side horizontal, still stretching, and lower heels (3); lower arms to sides (4).

Fig. 13.

From side straddle, bells overhead.

2. Bend trunk forward and swing bells between legs (1) Fig. 13; recover (2); bend trunk obliquely forward to the right and swing bells downward and upward on either side of body (3); recover (4); bend obliquely to the left, arms as in 3 (5); recover (6).

110　　　MANUAL OF PHYSICAL TRAINING.

From attention.

3. Hop to side straddle and raise bells to side horizontal (1); bend trunk forward and clasp right thigh with arms, right knee bent, left extended, (2) Fig. 14; recover position described under 1 (3); and recover attention (4). Repeat, alternating right and left.

FIG. 14.

4. Lunge sideward right and raise bells to side horizontal (1); bend trunk sideward right and swing left bell upward and right downward behind body (2); same position as in 1 (3); recover attention (4). Repeat, alternating on right and left.

5. Bend knees to squatting position and place bells on floor between feet (1); extend legs backward to leaning-rest (2); turn to the left about and assume the sitting position (3); turn right about and return to leaning-rest (4); to the squatting position (5); and recover attention (6). Repeat, alternating, turn to the right and left.
6. Hop to the side straddle position, arms stretched in side horizontal (1); twist trunk to the left (2); to the right (3); to the left (4); forward (5); and recover (6). Repeat, beginning on the right.

SIXTH SERIES.

This series is the same as the fifth series of the setting-up exercises, prescribed for trained soldiers.

CLUB EXERCISES.

The effect of thése exercises, when performed with light clubs, is chiefly a neural one, hence they are primary factors in the development of grace and coordination and rhythm. As they tend to supple the muscles and articulations of the shoulders and of the upper and fore arms and wrist, they are indicated in cases where there is a tendency toward what is ordinarily known as "muscle bound."

There is a great variety of movements with the clubs, but for the purposes of this manual the fundamental principles will suffice, and therefore only these are included.

The club exercises consist of *arm* and *wrist circles*, the former being divided into *extended* or *full-arm circles* and *bent* or *half-arm circles*. In the extended arm circle the shoulder is the pivot and in the bent arm circle the elbow.

These circles derive their designation from the direction in which the club moves with reference to a median vertical line running through the body; thus an *outward circle* is one in which the initial movement of the club is *away* from this line and an *inward circle* where that movement is *toward* it; a *forward circle* is one in which it moves to the front and a *backward* circle in which it moves to the rear. When both clubs move in the same plane, the direction is either *right* or *left*, *forward* or *backward*, and when they move in opposite directions the circles are either *inward* or *outward*.

The *starting position* from which these exercises are performed is assumed at the command:

1. Clubs to the starting position, 2. RAISE.

114   MANUAL OF PHYSICAL TRAINING.

At the command *raise* the clubs are brought to a vertical position by flexing the forearms well up to the upper arms without stiffness;

Fig. 1.

the club is in prolongation of the forearm, and the hands are at the height of and opposite the shoulders; the fingers grasp the neck of the club loosely with the thumbs partially extended in opposition to the fingers; the knob of the club projects beyond the little finger; the upper arms rest loosely against the sides of the body, and the distance between the hands is the same as the width of the chest, Fig. 1.

CLUB EXERCISES.

At the command: 1. Clubs, 2. DOWN, the clubs are lowered to the sides, arms extended.

Fig. 2.

SINGLE-ARM EXERCISES.

Extended arm circle outward. Fig. 2.
Extended arm circle inward.
Extended arm circle forward. Fig. 3.
Extended arm circle backward.
Command: 1. Extended right arm circle outward, 2. SWING, 3. HALT.
Continue at one, two.

116 MANUAL OF PHYSICAL TRAINING.

The right arm is extended overhead without stiffness and the club is circled away from the body; when it swings across the body the arm is flexed slightly at the elbow in order that the body does not become deranged. This rule is general.

Fig. 3.

The count should be given just as the club reaches the horizontal in its descent. This rule, too, is general.

In all club exercises it should be the endeavor of the men to keep the club in a plane parallel with the body throughout its movement.

At *halt* the starting position is resumed.

CLUB EXERCISES. 117

SINGLE BENT ARM EXERCISES.

Repeat the extended arm circles, substituting the word *bent* for the word *extended* in the command given above.

FIG. 4.

SINGLE-WRIST CIRCLES.

1. Wrist circle forward, inside or outside of arms. Fig. 4.
2. Wrist circle backward, inside or outside of arms.
3. Wrist circle inward, behind shoulders. Fig. 5.
4. Wrist circle outward, behind shoulders.
5. Horizontal wrist circle, inward or outward, over or under arms. Fig. 6.

Command: 1. Wrist circle right forward, 2. SWING, 3. HALT.
Continue at one, two.

Fig. 5.

Fig. 6.

MANUAL OF PHYSICAL TRAINING.

Double Extended Arm Circles.

In these exercises both clubs move simultaneously.
1. Double extended arm circle to the right.   Fig. 7.
2. Same, left.

Fig. 7.

3. Double extended arm circle forward.
4. Same, backward.
5. Double extended arm circle inward.   Fig. 8.
6. Same, outward.

CLUB EXERCISES. 121

Command: Double extended arm circle right, 2. SWING, 3. HALT. Continue at one, two.

In the double circles, to the right and left, the distance between the hands remains the same and the clubs should always be in prolongation of the arms. Execute above with double bent arm circles.

FIG. 8.

1. Double wrist circles forward, inside or outside of arms.
2. Same, backward.
3. Double wrist circles inward, behind shoulders. Fig. 9.
4. Same, outward.

122 MANUAL OF PHYSICAL TRAINING.

5. Double wrist circles forward, inside or outside of arms.
6. Same, backward.
7. Double horizontal wrist circles, right or left, over or under arms. Fig. 10.

Command: 1. Double wrist circles forward, 2. SWING, 3. HALT.

FIG. 9.

Continue at one, two.

In the wrist circles the fingers should be brought into play as much as possible and the elbow and shoulder joints should be relaxed.

Fig. 10.

124   MANUAL OF PHYSICAL TRAINING.

SINGLE ARM AND WRIST CIRCLE COMBINATION.

1. Single extended, or bent, arm circles outward with wrist circles behind shoulder in the same direction.   Fig. 11.

FIG. 11.

2. Same, inward.
3. Single extended, or bent, arm circles forward with wrist circle in the same direction.
4. Same, backward.

CLUB EXERCISES. 125

5. Single half bent arm circle inward and horizontal wrist circle inward over arm, the club moving across body. Fig. 12.
6. Single bent arm circle outward and horizontal wrist circle outward over arm, the club moving across the body.

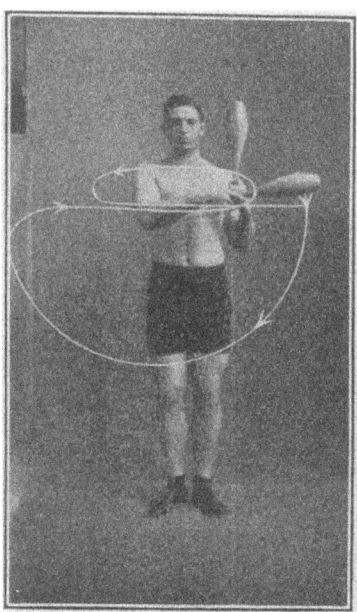

FIG. 12.

In the above exercises and in all that follow the description of the combination always constitutes the preparatory command; when this is too lengthy, however, the caution *ready* should precede the command swing.

MANUAL OF PHYSICAL TRAINING.

Double Arm and Wrist Combination.

1. Double extended, or bent arm, circles to the right and wrist circles behind shoulders in the same direction. Fig. 13.
2. Same to the left.

Fig. 13.

3. Double extended, or bent arm, circles inward and wrist circles in the same direction behind shoulders. Fig. 14.
4. Same, outward.
5. Double extended, or bent arm, circles forward with wrist circles in the same direction.
6. Same, backward.

CLUB EXERCISES.

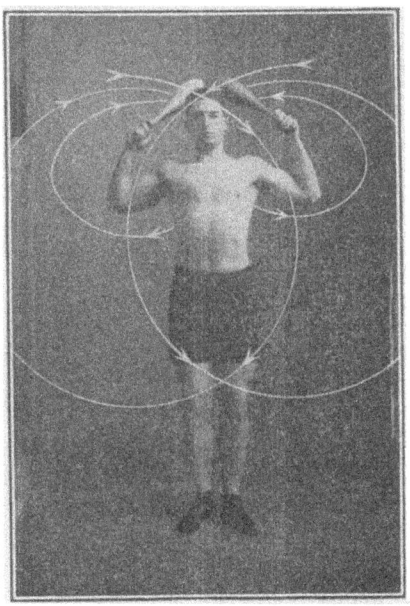

Fig. 14.

7. Double bent arm half circles inward, to side horizontal and horizontal wrist circles over arms inward.
8. Same arm and wrist circles moving outward.

Fig. 15.

9. Double bent arm half circle to the right with wrist circles over arms to the right.
10. Same, left.
11. Double arm circles to the right with wrist circles behind shoulders in the same direction, the right club leading by half a swing. "The Mill."
12. Same to the left.

CLUB EXERCISES.

13. Double arm circles inward with wrist circles behind shoulders in same direction; the right arm begins with the arm circle and the left with the wrist circle. Fig. 15.
14. Same, swinging clubs outward.

CLUB COMBINATION.

The best results are obtained by combining these simple movements into one combination, the swinging of which should be made the objective.

Each exercise is repeated four times.

1. Right extended arm circle outward.
2. Right bent arm circle outward.
3. Right bent arm circle outward with wrist circle behind shoulders in same direction.
4. ⎫
5. ⎬ Same with the left arm.
6. ⎭
7. Right extended arm circle inward.
8. Right bent arm circle inward.
9. Right bent arm circle inward with wrist circle behind shoulders in same direction.
10. ⎫
11. ⎬ Same with the left arm.
12. ⎭
13. Double extended arm circles right.
14. Double bent arm circles right.
15. Double extended arm circles left.
16. Double bent arm circles left.
17. Double extended arm circle inward (cross arms above).
18. Reverse at the horizontal and double extended arm circles outward (cross arms below).
19. Change to double bent arm circle outward with wrist circles behind shoulders in the same direction.

20. After the fourth wrist circle the clubs are brought forward overhead and the bent arm and wrist circles are reversed, now being inward.
21. After the fourth swing the left arm continues to circle inward as in 20; while the right club executes an additional wrist circle and then resumes the inward arm and wrist circles described under 20. This is the inward "right and left" movement, the right club being swung in a wrist circle behind the shoulder, while the left arm performs the arm circle in front of the body; the clubs alternating in the wrist and arm circles.
22. After the left wrist has performed the fourth circle inward behind the shoulder and the right arm is about to reach the horizontal on the right, the course of the clubs is reversed; the left wrist beginning the new movement with the outward wrist circle and the right club with the outward arm circle; the outward "right and left" movement, clubs alternating as in 21.
23. At the completion of the last outward wrist circle with the right club and the arm circle with the left, both clubs are joined at the right shoulder and swung in a double bent arm circle to the right, with wrist circles behind shoulders in the same direction.
24. After completing the last wrist circle to the right, the movement is reversed by swinging the right club over the head and the left over the shoulder, and both clubs are swung as in 23, to the left.
25. After the fourth wrist circle behind the shoulders to the left both clubs are swung in a half bent-arm circle from the left to the horizontal on the right, from where they are brought back to the left horizontal by circling the clubs to the left in wrist circles over the arms.

CLUB EXERCISES. 131

26. Upon completing the last wrist circle to the left, the movement is reversed by reversing the wrist circles from left to right and continuing as in 25 in the opposite direction.
27. After the fourth wrist circle from left to right, both clubs are swung in the double bent-arm circles to the right with the wrist circles in the same direction behind the shoulder; they are then swung downward with a double half-arm circle to the left horizontal and brought from there to the right horizontal by a horizontal wrist circle over the arms from left to right (26).
28. After the fourth wrist circle from the left to the right, the clubs are brought from the right horizontal to the left horizontal by means of a horizontal wrist circle and the entire combination (27) is swung from left to right.
29. When the clubs reach the left horizontal after the fourth horizontal circle from the right horizontal, they are swung in a bent-arm circle from left to right until they reach a point at the height of the shoulders; from here the left club is swung in a bent-arm circle forward and the right club describes an inner wrist circle behind the shoulders; after the completion of these circles the left club circles behind the shoulder and the right club circles forward in a bent-arm swing; this is the "forward right-and-left" movement, one club circling in a wrist circle while the other is describing the arm circle (21) only parallel with the sides of the body.
30. After swinging the combination four times on the right and the same number of times on the left, the clubs are joined on the right and swung in a double bent-arm circle forward with wrist circles to the right. As the clubs are extended forward, they are changed to the left side of the body and the same movement is taken on that side; alternate from right to left, swinging the combination four times on each side.

31. After the last circle on the left the clubs are brought to the starting position and the following movements are performed once:
1. Wrist circles forward on outside of arms.
2. Half-arm circles forward and backward.
3. Return to starting position.
4. Wrist circles forward outside of arms.
5. Wrist circles inside of arms, clubs coming in contact with arm pits. Return to starting position.
6. Wrist circles outside of arms.
7. Swing clubs downward as in 2.
8. Return to starting position as in 3.

Numbers indicate the counts in the last combination.

RIFLE EXERCISES.

The object of these exercises, which may also be performed with wands or bar bells, is to develop the muscles of the arms, shoulders, and back so that the men will become accustomed to the weight of the piece and learn to wield it with that "handiness" so essential to its successful use. When these exercises are combined with movements of the various other parts of the body, they serve as a splendid, though rather strenuous, method for the all-round development of the men. As the weight of the piece is considerable instructors are cautioned to be reasonable in their demands. Far better results are obtained if these exercises are performed at commands than when they are grouped and performed for spectacular purposes.

All the exercises start from the starting position, which is the low extended arm horizontal position in front of the body, arms straight; the right hand grasping the small of the stock and the left hand the barrel; the knuckles turned to the front and the distance between the hands slightly greater than the width of the shoulders. Fig. 1.

This position is assumed at the command: 1. Starting, 2. POSITION; at the command *position* the piece is brought to the port and lowered to the front horizontal snappily.

To recover the position of order, command: 1. Order, 2. ARMS; the piece is first brought to the port and then ordered.

Arm Exercises.

From the starting position (Fig. 1); all exercises are in two counts.

1. Raise piece to front extended arm horizontal.
2. Raise piece to high overhead, extended arm horizontal.
3. Raise piece to side horizontal, right or left. Fig. 2.
4. Raise piece to front perpendicular, right or left hand up. Fig. 3.
5. Raise piece to front bent arm horizontal, waist high.
6. Raise piece to front bent arm horizontal, shoulder high. Fig. 4.
7. Raise piece to rear bent arm horizontal, on shoulders, Fig. 5.
8. Raise piece to front bent arm horizontal, shoulder high, arms crossed, left over right or vice versa.
9. Raise piece to low side perpendicular, right or left, right or left hand up. Fig. 6.
10. Raise piece to high side perpendicular, right or left. Fig. 7.

    In the above exercises the movement begins at the command "EXERCISE" and is discontinued at "HALT."

From front bent arm horizontal, shoulder high:

11. Thrust piece forward, upward, downward or sideward, right or left.
12. Thrust piece upward from rear, bent arm horizontal.

From high extended arm horizontal:

13. Circle piece from right to left, or from left to right. Describe complete circle parallel with the front of the body.

RIFLE EXERCISES.

Fig. 1.

Fig. 2.

RIFLE EXERCISES.

Fig. 3.

138 MANUAL OF PHYSICAL TRAINING.

FIG. 4.

RIFLE EXERCISES. 139

FIG. 5.

140   MANUAL OF PHYSICAL TRAINING.

FIG. 6.

RIFLE EXERCISES. 141

Fig. 7.

ARM COMBINATIONS.

All of the following exercises consist of four movements, the third carrying the piece back to the first position, and the fourth to the starting position; in other words, the piece is carried back in reverse order at *three* and *four*.

1. Raise piece to high extended arm horizontal; flex to the bent arm horizontal in front of shoulders and return in reverse order.
2. Same as above, except that the piece is brought to the shoulders in rear of head.
3. Raise piece as in 1; lower to right horizontal, and return in reverse order.
4. Same, left.
5. Raise piece to front bent arm horizontal, shoulder high; thrust piece upward, and return in reverse order.
6. Same, thrusting piece forward or sideward right or left.
7. Raise piece to front extended arm perpendicular, right hand up; reverse bringing left hand up; reverse again and lower.
8. Raise piece to low side perpendicular, left hand up; change to high side perpendicular, right hand up; and return in reverse order.
9. Same on the left.
10. Raise piece to front extended arm horizontal; cross and bend arms to front bent arm horizontal right over left; and return in reverse order.
11. Raise piece to front bent arm horizontal, arms crossed, right over left; change by crossing left over right; reverse and down.

ARM, LEG, AND TRUNK COMBINATIONS.

From the starting position: All exercises in two counts.

1. Raise piece to front extended arm horizontal and bend knees quarter, half, or full.

RIFLE EXERCISES. 143

2. Raise piece to high extended arm horizontal and raise on toes.
3. Raise piece as in 2 and bend trunk forward.
4. Raise piece to rear bent arm horizontal on shoulders and bend trunk forward.
5. Raise piece to front perpendicular, left hand up, and bend trunk sideward right. Fig. 8.
6. Same to the left, right hand up.
7. Raise piece to high right side perpendicular and bend trunk sideward left.
8. Same, piece on the left, bending trunk to the right.

From front bent arm horizontal, shoulder high.

9. Thrust piece forward or upward and bend knees, quarter, half, or full.
10. Raise piece forward and upward and bend trunk forward.
11. Thrust piece sideward right and bend trunk sideward left.
12. Same reversed.
13. Thrust piece forward and twist body to the left or right.
14. Thrust piece upward and bend trunk backward.
15. Thrust piece upward and hop to side straddle.
16. Thrust piece forward or upward and lunge forward right or left.
17. Thrust piece upward or forward and lunge obliquely forward right or left.
18. Thrust piece sideward left and lunge sideward right or left.
19. Thrust piece upward and lunge backward.
20. Thrust piece downward lunge forward and bend body forward, Fig. 9.
21. Thrust piece upward; lunge backward and bend trunk backward. Fig. 10
22. Thrust piece side right and lunge and bend trunk sideward left. Fig. 11.

144   MANUAL OF PHYSICAL TRAINING.

Fig. 8.

RIFLE EXERCISES.

Fig. 9.

146   MANUAL OF PHYSICAL TRAINING.

FIG. 10.

Fig. 11.

MANUAL OF PHYSICAL TRAINING.

Rifle Drill Combination.

The following exercises consist of four movements, the third position always corresponding to the first position and the fourth

Fig. 12.

to the starting position. They have been grouped and arranged precisely like the setting-up combination, Fifth Lesson, prescribed for trained soldiers. When performed as a musical drill, the instructions laid down in that lesson are applicable here.

All exercises begin and end with the first or starting position; Fig. 1.

RIFLE EXERCISES. 149

First Group.

First Exercise.

Fig. 13.

Counts.
1—2. Raise piece to bent arm front horizontal, shoulder high, and stride forward right, Fig. 12;
3—4. Face to the left on both heels and extend piece upward, Fig. 13;
5—6. Resume first position;
7—8. Resume starting position.
    Repeat left, right, left, right.

150 MANUAL OF PHYSICAL TRAINING.

Second Exercise.

Fig. 14.

Counts.
1—2. Raise piece to extended high horizontal, and stride sideward right, Fig. 14;
3—4. Bend right knee and lower piece to left horizontal, Fig. 15;
5—6. Resume first position;
7—8. Resume starting position.
  Repeat left, right left.

Fig. 15.

152 MANUAL OF PHYSICAL TRAINING.

Third Exercise.

FIG. 16.

Counts.
1—2. Raise piece to high side perpendicular on the left, left hand up, and stride backward right, Fig. 16;
3—4. Face about on heels and swing piece down and up to high side perpendicular on the right, Fig. 17;
5—6. Resume first position;
7—8. Resume starting position.
    Repeat left, right, left.

RIFLE EXERCISES.

FIG. 17.

154   MANUAL OF PHYSICAL TRAINING.

Fourth Exercise.

FIG. 18.

Counts.
1—2. Raise piece to extended high horizontal, and stride obliquely forward right, Fig. 18;
3—4. Face about on heels and lower piece to horizontal on shoulders, Fig. 19;
5—6. Resume first position;
7—8. Resume starting position.
   Repeat left, right, left.

RIFLE EXERCISES. 155

Fig. 19.

156 MANUAL OF PHYSICAL TRAINING.

SECOND GROUP.

First Exercise.

FIG. 20.

Counts.
1—2. Lower piece to front extended horizontal and bend trunk forward, Fig. 20;
3—4. Lunge obliquely forward right and raise piece to right oblique, left hand at shoulder, Fig. 21;
5—6. Resume first position;
7—8. Resume starting position.
    Repeat left, right, left.

RIFLE EXERCISES.

Fig. 21.

158   MANUAL OF PHYSICAL TRAINING.

Second Exercise.

Fig. 22.

Counts.
1—2. Raise piece to high perpendicular on the left, left hand up, and bend trunk sideward right, Fig. 22;
3—4. Lunge sideward right and swing piece down and up to right high perpendicular, right hand up, Fig. 23;
5—6. Resume first position;
7—8. Resume starting position.
    Repeat left, right, left.

Fig. 23.

160 MANUAL OF PHYSICAL TRAINING.

Third Exercise.

FIG. 24.

Counts.
1—2. Raise piece to high extended arm horizontal and bend trunk
 backward, Fig. 24;
3—4. Lunge forward right, and swing piece to side horizontal, left
 hand to the rear, Fig. 25;
5—6. Resume first position;
7—8. Resume starting position.
 Repeat left. right, left.

RIFLE EXERCISES.

Fig. 25.

162   MANUAL OF PHYSICAL TRAINING.

Fourth Exercise.

Fig. 26.

Counts.
1—2. Raise piece to right high perpendicular and side step position left, Fig. 26;
3—4. Lunge sideward left and swing piece to left high perpendicular, Fig. 27;
5—6. Resume first position;
7—8. Resume starting position.
      Repeat left, right, left.

RIFLE EXERCISES.

Fig. 27.

164   MANUAL OF PHYSICAL TRAINING.

THIRD GROUP.

First Exercise.

FIG. 28.

Counts.
1—2. Raise piece to front bent horizontal, arms crossed, left over right; lunge sideward right and bend trunk sideward right, Fig. 28;
3—4. Extend right knee and bend trunk to the left, bending left knee and recrossing arms, left over right, Fig. 29;
5—6. Resume first position;
7—8. Resume starting position.
   Repeat left, right, left.

RIFLE EXERCISES.

Fig. 29.

166   MANUAL OF PHYSICAL TRAINING.

Second Exercise.

Fig. 30.

Counts.
1—2. Raise piece to bent arm horizontal; face right and lunge forward right and bend trunk forward, Fig. 30;
3—4. Raise trunk and turn to the left on both heels and extend piece overhead, Fig. 31;
5—6. Resume first position;
7—8. Resume starting position.
   Repeat left, right, left.

RIFLE EXERCISES. 167

FIG. 31.

168 MANUAL OF PHYSICAL TRAINING.

Third Exercise.

FIG. 32.

Counts.
1—2. Raise piece to left high horizontal; lunge forward right, Fig. 32;
3—4. Bend trunk forward and lower piece to low front horizontal, Fig. 33;
5—6. Resume first position;
7—8. Resume starting position.
   Repeat left, right, left.

RIFLE EXERCISES. 169

Fig. 33.

170 MANUAL OF PHYSICAL TRAINING.

Fourth Exercise.

FIG. 34.

Counts.
1—2. Raise piece to high extended horizontal and hop to side straddle position, Fig. 34;
3—4. Bend trunk forward and swing piece to extended low horizontal, left hand between legs, right hand forward, Fig. 35;
5—6. Resume first position;
7—8. Resume starting position.
      Repeat left, right, left.

RIFLE EXERCISES.

Fig. 35.

CLIMBING.

Exercises on Single Vertical Pole.

Unless otherwise directed, all exercises begin from and end in the position of attention.

First Series.

1. To the extended-arm-hang, LEAP, DROP. Fig. 1.

    At *leap* the soldier springs upward, grasps the pole with his hands high enough to clear the floor with his toes. While hanging, his arms are extended, head erect, back arched slightly, legs closed tightly, knees straight, feet together, and toes depressed.

    At *drop* he lights on his toes, bends his knees to half-bend position; body erect, and allows his hands to slip down the pole until his arms are horizontal; then, as he extends his knees, he drops his arms smartly to his sides, and resumes the position of attention. Repeat this exercise until all can execute it faultlessly.

    The following exercises are executed from the extended-arm-hang described above:

2. Repeat extended-arm-hang and drop several times without pausing.
3. Straddle and close legs.
4. Cross left leg over right and reverse.
5. Raise and lower heel or heels.
6. Raise and lower knee or knees.

174 MANUAL OF PHYSICAL TRAINING.

FIG. 1.

CLIMBING.

Second Series.

FIG. 2.

1. Grasp pole between knees and feet, legs straight.
2. Grasp pole between knees and raise heels.
3. Raise knees and grasp pole between them.
4. Raise knee and then extend leg forward.
5. Raise knees and then extend legs forward, pole between legs. Fig. 2.

Fig. 3.

6. Climbing-clinch, right (left) leg in front. Fig. 3.

In this position the legs are crossed about the pole; right heel is pressed against the front, and left instep against the rear of pole; legs are extended.

CLIMBING.

Third Series.

FIG. 4.

1. Assume above position and change left leg in front.
2. Assume various leg positions and change to climbing-clinch.
3. Assume climbing-clinch and change to various leg positions, and return to climbing clinch.
4. Leap to extended-arm-hang and draw body to bent-arm-hang. Fig. 4.
5. Assume various leg positions, and change from extended to bent-arm-hang.

Fourth Series.

Fig. 5.

1. Climbing-clinch and remove and replace right (left) hand.
2. Climbing-clinch and raise knees. Fig. 5.
3. Climbing-clinch, raise knees and release hand.
4. Leap to the bent-arm-hang.
5. Repeat several times without pausing.
6. Execute the exercises described under previous lessons.

CLIMBING.

Fifth Series.

Fig. 6.

1. Climb, hand over hand. Fig. 6.

    In the ordinary climb the legs should be depended upon to do most of the work, the arms being used chiefly to hold the weight of the body while the legs are being raised. It is essential, therefore, that the men learn to use the legs properly. In climbing the knees are raised as high as possible, the pole being firmly clinched by the knees, the ankles and the feet; the body is then extended upward from the knees and the hands advanced.

Variety may be given these exercises by climbing:

2. Hand after hand, one hand leading.
3. Both hands simultaneously.
4. Alternating the climbing-clinch, from right forward to left forward.

Sixth Series.

Leap to bent-arm-hang and climb:

1. Hand over hand, without use of legs.
2. Hand after hand, without use of legs.
3. Climbing with use of legs for speed.
4. Climbing without use of legs for speed.

Exercises on Swinging Pole.

Seventh Series.

At *Ready* the soldier will grasp the pole in the right hand and move backward until the pole is held at the height of the shoulder. At *Go* he will run forward, moving hands upward on the pole as he runs, and jump into the different positions enumerated below just as the pole begins to swing upward on the opposite side. Fig. 7.

1. Leap to extended-arm-hang and drop at end of first rear swing.
2. Same, dropping at end of second, third, or fourth swing.
3. Same, assuming any of the leg positions.
4. Same, dropping at end of second or third downward swing, facing starting point.
5. Leap to bent-arm-hang; dropping at end of first, second, or third swing.
6. Leap to bent-arm-hang with legs in climbing-clinch.
7. Leap to climbing-clinch and climb hand over hand, hand after hand, or with both hands simultaneously.

FIG. 7.

182   MANUAL OF PHYSICAL TRAINING.

Exercises on Two Poles.

Eighth Series.

Fig. 8.

1. Leap to extended-arm-hang. Fig. 8.
2. Same, raising heels or knees, straddling, crossing or raising legs.
3. Leap to extended-arm-hang, change to climbing-clinch on one pole, hands on both.
4. Same, changing both hands to same pole, legs to the other.
5. Leap to extended-arm-hang and change to inner-climbing-clinch on both poles. Knees in front of the poles; feet twisted about the poles from the outisde. Fig. 9.

CLIMBING.

Fig. 9.

MANUAL OF PHYSICAL TRAINING.

Ninth Series.

FIG. 10.

1. Leap to bent-arm-hang. Fig. 10.
2. Leap to bent-arm-hang, with various leg positions.
3. Leap to bent-arm-hang, with inner-climbing-clinch.
4. Leap to bent-arm-hang, swinging legs backward and forward.
5. Leap to bent-arm-hang, swinging legs and turning over to the stand.

CLIMBING.

Tenth Series.

Fig. 11.

From the stand:
1. Leap to inverted-hang. Fig. 11.
2. Leap and turn-over to the stand.
3. Leap to inverted-hang, straddle legs and press them against pole.
4. Leap to inverted-inner climbing-clinch on both poles.
5. Climb inner-climbing-clinch, hand and leg on same side moving together. Fig. 12.
6. Same as 5, but hand and leg on opposite side moving together.

Eleventh Series.

Fig. 12.

1. Climb hand after hand without the use of the legs.
2. Climb, moving both hands simultaneously.
3. Swing legs backward and forward and climb hand after hand at end of forward swing.
4. Execute the various exercises described in two poles while the poles are swinging.

CLIMBING.

SINGLE AND DOUBLE ROPES.

With few exceptions the various exercises described above may be performed on the ropes. Considerable difficulty is added to the rope climbing on account of its flexibility.

SINGLE INCLINED POLE OR ROPE.

Twelfth Series.

1. Stand under and facing low end of the rope and leap to extended-arm-hang. Fig. 13.
2. Same, leaping to bent-arm-hang.
3. Stand under and facing high end of rope and leap to extended-arm-hang. Fig. 14.
4. Same to bent-arm-hang.
5. Stand sidewise, facing rope, the rope parallel with front of body, and leap to extended or bent-arm-hang.
6. Stand under facing low end of rope and leap to extended or bent arm-hang, right leg (or left) thrown over rope, other leg extended. Fig. 15.
7. Same as above, both legs crossed over rope. Fig. 16.

Thirteenth Series.

1. Same as above, leap to arm-hang, legs crossed over rope, and climb upward.
2. Assume position as above and climb upward, legs being thrown over rope alternately.
3. Stand as above and leap to either arm-hang and climb upward hand over hand without use of legs.
4. Stand facing high end of rope and climb upward hand over hand.

Ropes or poles should be inclined at an angle of about 45 degrees.

Fig. 13.

FIG. 14.

Fig. 15.

FIG. 16.

JUMPING EXERCISES.

BROAD.

First Series.

The preliminary exercises in jumping may be practiced by large squads and at command. These exercises are valuable because the men will learn to jump in proper form. The class may be divided into squads of four, six, or eight men.

The first squad will take its place in front of the class and execute the following exercises from one end of the gymnasium to the other:
1. Ordinary standing jump, coming to attention after every jump.

> At *Ready* the squad will raise arms forward shoulder high and raise body on toes, Fig. 1; at *Leap* the arms are swung to the rear without deranging the position of the body, and the knees are slightly bent, Fig. 2; as the arms come forward again the knees are extended and the body is thrust from the floor and advanced about a yard. During the flight the feet are closed and depressed, the legs are extended, the body is well arched, arms are forward, and the head is erect. Fig. 3. In alighting the toes strike the floor first, the knees are well bent and extended, the arms are dropped, and the position of attention is smartly resumed.
>
> Repeat at commands *Ready, Leap.*

FIG. 1.   FIG. 2.

FIG. 3.

2. Continuous broad jumps.

Execute precisely as in 1, except that there is no pause between the jumps, every jump after the first being made from the bent-knee position; the arms continue to swing back and forth with every jump.

Continue at command *Leap*, given just as the toes strike the floor, and discontinue at the command *Halt*.

The entire class may take part in these exercises, 1 and 2, the squads following each other at intervals of two or three jumps, and breaking away to the right and left when the end of the gymnasium has been reached and reassembling at the starting point.

In the following exercises a take-off and mattress should be used. As the object is form rather than distance, the jump should not be more than from 5 to 7 feet. In all exercises the preliminary position is the same as in 1. The commands are *Ready, Leap;* the succeeding man takes the place of the jumper without command; the jumper joins the rear of the squad.

3. Jump from both feet and land on both feet.
4. Same, turning right or left, or right or left about.
5. Same as in 3, raising knees during the flight.
6. Same as in 3, landing on one foot.
7. Hop-jump from one foot and land on both.
8. Same, landing on opposite foot.
9. Same, landing on same foot.

Second Series.

1. Stride-jump, landing on both feet.

    The preliminary position for the stride-jump is as follows: One foot on edge of take-off; the other, resting on toes, is placed to the rear of the jumping foot; arms forward. In executing the jump the arms are swung downward and then to the front and the leg in the rear is swung forward.
2. Same as in 1, with turns.
3. Standing broad jump for distance.

JUMPING EXERCISES. 197

4. Walk, increasing the pace as the take-off is neared, and execute the various jumps described under 2. Distance, 6 to 10 feet.
5. Run, increasing the pace as the take-off is neared, and execute the jumps described under above series and the first three of this series. Distance 8 to 10 feet.
6. Run backward toward take-off, turn about without decreasing the pace, at half the distance, and stride-jump. This is the ordinary broad jump.

Third Series.

1. Run forward toward take-off, turn all the way around and jump.
2. Run backward toward take-off and turn once and a half around and jump.
3. Run forward and turn twice around and jump.
4. Run forward, turn once to the left and immediately to the right and jump.
5. Run backward, turn facing take-off, run several steps and turn around once and jump.
6. Run backward and continue to turn as often as possible and jump.

Fourth Series.

1. Run forward and pick up a boxing glove or other article placed half way between starting point and take-off, without decreasing the pace, and jump.
2. Turn, pick up the glove, and jump.
3. Turn, pick up the glove, turn again, and jump.
4. Run, imitate a stumble half way to the take-off, and jump.
   To imitate a stumble, run forward at a good pace, lean forward quickly, and endeavor to touch the floor with the hands; gather as quickly as possible and jump.
5. Combine the turns with the stumble.
6. Running broad-jump for distance.

High Jumping.

Fifth Series.

In these exercises it is best not to use a take-off board. The stick for these exercises should be placed about 30 inches from the floor. Arms are swung overhead.

1. Face the stick and jump forward from both feet.
2. Same, with turns to the right or left.
3. Same, grasping toes with hands for a moment, with one or both hands.
4. Standing with right or left side turned to stick, jump sideward from both feet.
5. Same as in 4, jumping as in 2.
6. Same as in 4, jumping as in 3.

Sixth Series.

1. Stand as in 4 in Fifth Series, and stride-jump over stick, without turning.
2. Same as 1, turning away from the bar during the flight.
3. Same as 2, turning about during the flight.
4. Face the stick and hop over it from one foot, landing on both.
5. Same, landing on the same foot.
6. Standing high-jump for height.

Seventh Series.

Execute the various high jumps described, first from a walk and then from a run.

1. Running high-jump for height.

   The men should be permitted to select their own style of run, jump, and take-off for these exercises.
2. Standing or running broad-high jump.

   In this jump the take-off and the jumping standards are used; the take-off being moved back and the jumping stick raised after every jump.

APPARATUS—SIDE AND LONG HORSE EXERCISES.

APPARATUS.

The object of apparatus work is described under paragraph 2, to which the attention of instructors is called.

The terms "cross" and "side," as used in the text with reference to the various exercises, denote the relation between the longest line of the apparatus and the line running from shoulder to shoulder of the soldier. Thus, a "*side rest*" is one where the line from shoulder to shoulder of the soldier is parallel to the longest line of the apparatus. In the case of the horse this line is from croup to neck. A "*cross rest*" is one where the line of the shoulders is perpendicular to the longest line of the apparatus.

In all dismounts from any apparatus the body invariably alights on the toes, the knees being well bent and separated so the point of the knees is directly over the toes; the body is erect on the hips, head up. From this position the knees are extended quickly and smartly to the position of attention. The entire motion from the moment the toes strike the ground till the position of attention is assumed is a continuous one.

When exercising on the parallel bars, the horses, or the vaulting bars the hand nearest the apparatus rests on it momentarily while dismounting, but it is lowered to the side smartly when the knees are being extended. The hand farthest from the apparatus is lowered to the side. When the front of the body is turned to the apparatus in dismounting, both hands rest on it.

The preparatory command for all exercises on apparatus is *Ready;* the command of execution, depending upon the character of the movement, is *Leap, Mount,* or *Vault*. To alight from any apparatus command *Dismount* or *Drop*.

VAULTING HORSE EXERCISES.

SIDE HORSE EXERCISES.

Exercises when the take-off is placed at the side of the horse are known as side horse exercises.

The horse is placed in such a position that the neck is on the left of the take-off.

As a rule these exercises are executed with the pommels fixed; the height of these pommels being equal to the height of the breast of the average man of the squad.

The parts of the horse to which reference is made in the description of the exercises are: The neck, saddle, croup, and the pommels. The pommel between the neck and the saddle is known as the front and that between the saddle and the croup as the rear pommel.

The side nearest the take-off is the near and the opposite side the off-side.

Horse exercises are intended to specially develop activity, agility, and gracefulness, which can, however, be obtained only by constantly insisting that every movement, no matter how simple, be accurately and smartly executed.

These exercises are of special value in the training of mounted troops, as they teach men the proper coordination of those muscles that are employed in riding.

FIRST SERIES.

All of these exercises should first be executed from a stand on the take-off, and later from a run. When executed from a run, the soldier leaps from one foot from the floor, lands on the take-off on

APPARATUS

both feet, and immediately proceeds to jump upon or over the horse from both feet.

Position of attention on the take-off:

1. To extended-side-rest, Ready, LEAP, DISMOUNT. Fig. 1.

    At *Ready* the soldier grasps the pommels firmly and raises his body on the toes, arms straight, body erect; at *Leap* he bends his knees slightly and springs upward to the rest on the hands, thighs against the horse. In this position his head is erect, chest out, shoulders square, arms straight, legs extended and closed tightly, feet together, and toes depressed. At *Dismount* he allows his body to drop backward without bending his arms and alights on his toes, bending his knees slightly as he does so, and dropping his arms smartly to his sides as he extends his knees.

2. Leap to extended-side-rest as before, dismount, and, without releasing hands, spring back to the rest again. Repeat several times.

Leap to the extended-side-rest and execute the following:

3. Raise and lower heel or heels.
4. Raise and lower leg backward.
5. Raise and lower leg sideward.
6. Turn body right (left).
7. Turn body right (left) and then about.
8. Kneel on one knee, other leg extended downward.
9. Kneel on both knees.
10. Squat on one foot, other leg extended downward.
11. Squat on both feet. Fig. 2.
12. Kneel on one knee, other leg extended backward horizontally. Fig. 3.

Fig. 1.

APPARATUS.

Fig. 2.

204   MANUAL OF PHYSICAL TRAINING.

FIG. 3.

APPARATUS. 205

SECOND SERIES.

FIG. 4.

Except when otherwise indicated, the dismount will be to the take-off.

1. Leap to straddle-stand, feet outside of pommels, legs extended, hands retaining grip on pommels. Fig. 4.
2. Leap to straddle-mount on croup, facing front, i. e., facing neck. Fig. 5.
3. Same on neck, facing croup.
4. Same in saddle, swing leg over neck, facing croup.

206 MANUAL OF PHYSICAL TRAINING.

FIG. 5.

5. Same in saddle, swinging leg over croup, facing neck.
6. Same on neck, swing right leg over neck, facing neck.
7. Same in saddle, swinging right leg over front pommel, facing neck.
8. Same in saddle, swinging left leg over rear pommel, facing croup.
9. Leap to side-mount, facing take-off.   Fig. 6.

APPARATUS.

Third Series.

Fig. 6.

In the following exercises the dismount will be on the off-side:
1. Execute the straddle-mounts and dismount, facing the horse.
2. Leap to squatting-mount on both feet, and jump forward.
3. Leap to same position, feet outside of pommels, and jump forward.
4. Leap to straddle-stand, feet outside of pommels, and jump forward.
5. Leap to kneeling-mount on both knees and jump forward.
6. Mount on croup, facing front, raise leg backward and mount in saddle, facing rear, and dismount on off-side.
7. Same from neck to saddle.
8. Same from croup to neck.

Fourth Series.

1. Execute the above mount, raising the leg forward over the horse and then circling the other leg forward to the mount.
2. Mount on croup, facing front; place hands behind the body, swing legs forward and change to mount in saddle, then to neck and straddle over neck to position of attention.
3. Mount on croup, facing rear; place hands in front of body and swing legs backward and change to saddle, then to neck, and swing off backward to position of attention.
4. Mount on croup, facing rear, with left hand grasping rear pommel; twist trunk to mount on left thigh and circle right leg to mount in saddle, facing rear; dismount on offside. Same to neck.
5. Mount on croup, facing rear; execute 4; then grasping front pommel with right hand twist trunk to mount on right thigh and circle left leg to mount on neck, facing rear.
6. Mount on croup, facing neck; raise left leg forward to cross-thigh-mount, then circle right leg forward to right-thigh-mount in saddle, facing take-off; then circle left leg forward to straddle-mount on neck.
7. Same from neck to saddle and from there to croup.
8. Mount on croup, facing neck; change left leg as in 6, and circle right leg forward to straddle-mount in saddle, facing croup; then raise right leg forward to the cross-thigh-mount and circle the left leg to the straddle-mount on croup, facing neck.
9. Same changes from neck to saddle and back to neck.

APPARATUS.

FIFTH SERIES.

1. Leap and pivot backward to straddle-mount on croup, facing rear. Fig. 7.

    In the pivoting exercises one leg remains pressed against the side of the horse, acting as a pivot, while the other leg describes a circle backward or forward around it, the body turning with the circling leg. Thus, in the above exercise, the right, which is used as a pivot, is pressed against the horse in line with the rear pommel, while the left leg, raised as nearly horizontal as possible, describes a half circle backward over the croup, the body turning to the left.
2. Same exercise to the mount on the neck, facing front.
3. Leap to side-back-rest and pivot forward to straddle-mount on croup or neck, facing saddle. Fig. 8.
4. Leap and circle right leg over rear pommel and mount in saddle, facing offside, and pivot, circling left leg to straddle-mount on croup, facing front.
5. Same, circling right leg over front pommel and pivot, circling left leg to mount on neck, facing rear.
6. Same, circling right leg over front pommel and pivot, circling left leg to mount on croup, facing front.
7. Same, circling left leg over rear pommel and pivot, right leg to mount on neck, facing rear.
8. Place right hand on front pommel, leap and circle right leg over rear pommel, face left-about and pivot, circling right leg to mount on croup, facing front.
9. Place left hand on rear pommel, circle left leg over front pommel, face right-about and pivot, circling right leg to mount on neck.

210 MANUAL OF PHYSICAL TRAINING.

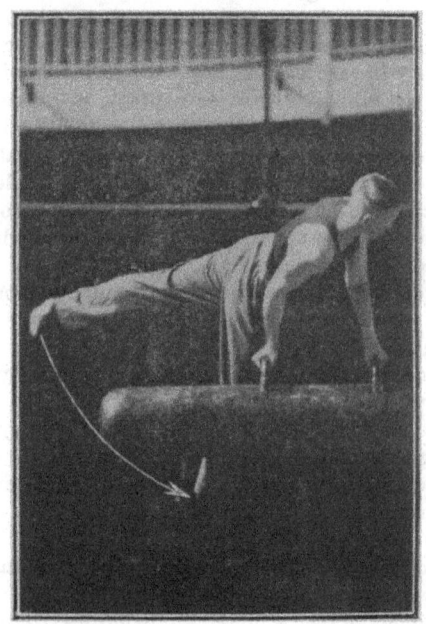

Fig. 7.

APPARATUS. 211

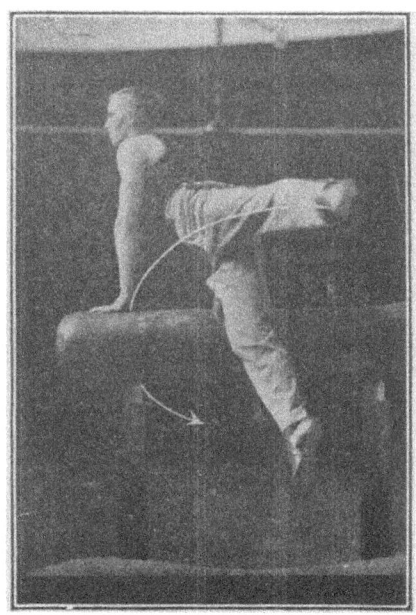

FIG. 8.

212 MANUAL OF PHYSICAL TRAINING.

Sixth Series.

These exercises are executed while mounted on the horse, and are used to change the direction of the mount, the mount itself, or as a means to dismounting. They may be executed backward, forward or sideward, the turns being to the right or left about.

Fig. 9.

1. Leap to straddle-mount on croup, facing front; grasp rear pommel with both hands, knuckles up; swing legs backward to leaning-rest, arms extended and legs resting against croup end of horse, cross the legs, right under left, face about and mount, facing rear; straddle off over croup. Fig. 9.

APPARATUS. 213

2. Repeat above exercise gradually, making the pause in the leaning-rest shorter, until the men can execute the *shears* by touching the horse with the legs for a moment only.
3. Swing legs backward and back-shears. Fig. 10.

In this and in the following exercises the men must be taught that the success of this and all of the following exercises depends upon the position of the legs and the turns of the

FIG. 10.

body. The legs must remain extended and be swung high enough to clear the horse; then as they are being crossed the body must be turned quickly.
4. Repeat these exercises on the neck; and then in the saddle.
5. Mount on croup, facing rear; grasp the rear pommel with both hands, knuckles turned away from the body, and swing legs forward as high as possible, lifting buttocks from the horse.

214   MANUAL OF PHYSICAL TRAINING.

6. Same mount; swing legs and raise buttocks as before, and execute *front shears*. Fig. 11.

FIG. 11.

In this exercise it is essential to swing forcibly enough to raise the body from the horse and as the legs reach the highest point the body is turned about quickly, being supported by one arm only while turning. If the turn is to the left about, the left hand remains on the pommel, while the right is released the instant the turn begins. The men must be cautioned that it is in the turn and not in the crossing of the legs that the "knack" of the exercise lies.

7. Mount to side-straddle in saddle, facing off-side, swing right leg over front or rear pommel; swing legs sideward left, and execute *side-shears*. Fig. 12.

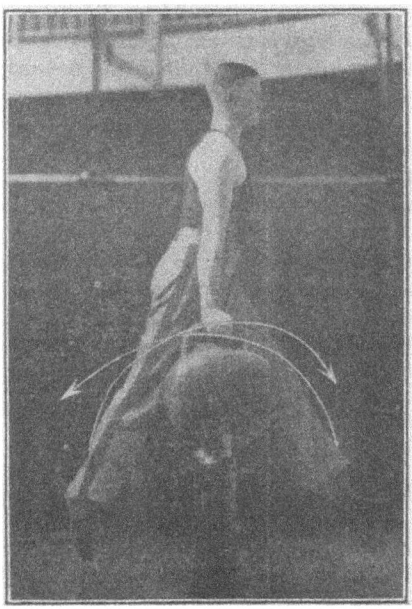

FIG. 12.

As the legs are swung to the left, the left hand is raised and the legs without bending are changed, the right to the rear and the left forward and the mount in the saddle is resumed with the left leg forward; the body is not turned.
8. Side-shears on the right, from mount with left leg in saddle.
9. From the take-off swing right leg over rear pommel and immediately execute 8.
10. Same, left leg over front pommel.

Seventh Series.

CIRCLES.

These exercises may be executed from the take-off, or from the extended-arm-rest. With beginners the circles should be first taken from the take-off and later from the take-off and concluding in the extended-arm-rest; then from the extended-arm-rest and concluding in that rest.

Single circles are executed with one and double circles with both legs. A single circle is said to be *inward* when it begins under the hand on the same side; *outward*, when it begins under the opposite hand. From the backward rest, this is reversed.

In the execution of these exercises the men must be cautioned to keep the arms extended and the weight well forward over the horse, especially when the leg moves backward; the leg is extended, and the body must not be allowed to turn. Proper cadence in order to shift the weight from hand to hand at the proper moment will do much toward a successful execution.

Single Circles.

1. Half circle right leg under left hand, and circle back under right.
2. Same, with left leg.
3. Half circle right leg under left hand, and circle back under left.
4. Same, with left leg.
5. Half circle right leg under right hand, and back under left.
6. Same, with left leg.
7. Half circle right leg under left hand, and back under right.
8. Same, with left leg.

APPARATUS.

EIGHTH SERIES.

9. Half circle right leg under right hand, then left under left hand, to side-mount, facing off-side, swing legs forward and dismount.
10. Half circle right leg under left hand, left leg under left hand, to mount and dismount as in 9.
11. Circle right leg inward, complete circle without pausing. Fig. 13.
12. Same, left.
13. Circle right leg outward, complete circle without pausing. Fig. 14.
14. Same, left.

NINTH SERIES.

Double Circles and Squatting Exercises.

1. Half-double-circle right, both legs under right hand, to back-rest in saddle, swing-off forward.
2. Same, left.
3. Half-double-circle right to back-rest; and half-double-circle backward right to take-off.
4. Same, left.
5. Same, forward on right and backward on left.
6. Same, forward on left and backward on right.

TENTH SERIES.

7. Squat right leg forward between arms to cross straddle and backward to take-off.
8. Same, with left.
9. Squat forward with right, then with left leg, and swing-off.
10. Squat forward with right, then backward with right and forward with left, and repeat.
11. Squat forward with both feet to side-mount, and swing-off.
12. Same, to back-rest, then backward to take-off.

218   MANUAL OF PHYSICAL TRAINING.

FIG. 13.

APPARATUS.

FIG. 14.

220 MANUAL OF PHYSICAL TRAINING.

ELEVENTH SERIES.

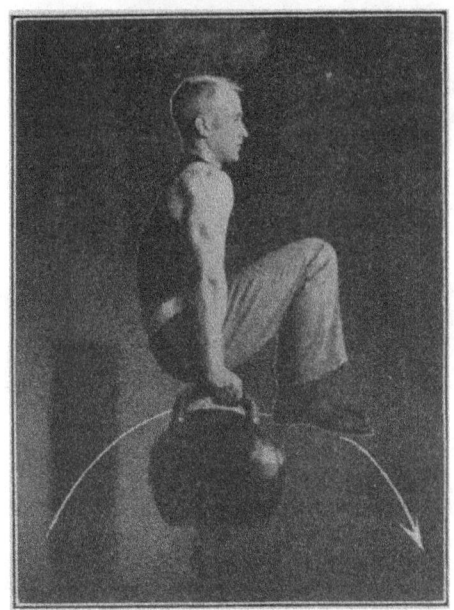

FIG. 15.

1. Squatting-vault. Fig. 15.
2. Squatting-vault with horizontal extension; legs are extended horizontally.
3. Squatting-vault with vertical extension; legs are extended downward.
4. Flank-vault, right and left. Fig. 16.
5. Rear-vault, right and left. Fig. 17.
6. Front-vault, right and left. Fig. 18.
7. Straddle-vault. Fig. 19.
8. The above vaults with turns.

Fig. 16.

Fig. 17.

Fig. 18.

Fig. 19.

APPARATUS.

LONG HORSE EXERCISES.

FIRST SERIES.

The horse is placed lengthwise, the pommels being removed and the height of the horse being the same as in the side horse exercises.

All exercises are similar to the side horse exercises; when detailed explanations are omitted, instructors will find them under same headings in the side horse exercises.

1. Leap to momentary cross-rest, hands on croup of horse, and dismount; thighs do not touch horse.
2. Leap to side rest on croup, facing right or left; fingers forward well over opposite side of horse. Dismount facing horse. Fig. 20.
3. Leap to straddle-mount on croup, facing front; dismount facing horse by swinging leg backward.
4. Same mount; dismount facing horse, by swinging leg forward.
5. Same mount; dismount facing front, by swinging both legs forward.
6. Same mount; dismount facing front, by swinging both legs backward.
7. Same mount; dismount facing rear, by pivoting leg forward.
8. Same mount; change by raising leg forward to oblique mount and pivoting other leg forward to mount, facing rear.
9. Execute above mounts and changes by leaping to straddle-mount in saddle.
10. Mount on croup, facing rear, leg is swung forward over the croup.
11. Leap to straddle-mount on neck; straddle over neck and dismount.

FIG. 20.

APPARATUS.

Second Series.
Kneeling-mounts.

Fig. 21.

1. Leap to side-kneeling-mount on croup, on one or both knees, facing left or right, and dismount backward. Fig. 21.
2. Leap as in 1, on both knees, and jump forward with assistance from hands.
3. Same as in 2, but jumping off without using hands.
4. Same as 3, jumping off with quarter or half turn.

5. Same as 2, kneeling on one knee only, other leg in rear of horse.
6. Leap to kneeling-mount as in 2, jump, with assistance of hands, to standing position on horse, and jump off forward or backward.
7. Same as in 6, without using hands.
8. Leap to side-kneeling-mount on both knees; jump off forward, facing about, and repeat the exercise again without pausing.
9. Leap to side-kneeling-mount; jump off forward, face about; leap to squatting-mount on horse, and jump off forward.
10. Same mount as 9; jump to standing position on horse; jump off forward with half turn; squat to standing to position on horse and jump off forward.

Third Series.

Squatting-mounts and shears.

1. Leap to cross-squatting-mount on croup, on one or both feet, facing front, dismount to take-off. Fig. 22.
2. Squat to standing position on croup, facing front; dismount right or left, without or with turn.
3. Leap to side squatting-mount on croup on one or both feet, facing right or left, and dismount forward or backward.
4. Squat to standing-position on croup, facing right or left; jump off forward.
5. Leap to cross-squatting-mount on croup; (Fig. 22) extend legs and body forward to leaning-rest, and drop off sideward. Fig. 23.
6. Same mount as 5, straddling over neck from leaning-rest.
7. Same mount as 5, extend body and legs and throw hands forward to rest on neck and straddle off at once.

APPARATUS.

FIG. 22.

230　　　MANUAL OF PHYSICAL TRAINING.

Fig. 23.

APPARATUS.

FOURTH SERIES.

1. Leap to standing position on croup, facing front; bend body forward and leap off with straddle over neck.
2. Leap to straddle-mount on croup or saddle, facing front and back-shears.
3. Same mount, and repeat shears several times.
4. Same mount, and front-shears.
5. Repeat several times.
6. Straddle-mount on croup or saddle, facing front; leaning-rest and back-shears.
7. Same mount, leaning-rest; part legs and drop to saddle; change hands behind body and front-shears. Repeat from leaning-rest.
8. Same mount; leaning-rest; drop as in 7; front-shears to straddle-mount, and repeat front-shears from straddle-mount at once.

FIFTH SERIES.

Pivot-mounts.

1. Leap to side-rest on croup on left side and pivot backward to straddle-mount in saddle facing front. Fig. 24.
2. Same, from side-rest on left side.
3. Leap and pivot-mount on right side at once.
4. Same, left.
5. Leap to straddle-mount on croup, facing left, right leg forward; and pivot left leg forward to mount in saddle, facing rear.
6. Same, left.
7. Leap to straddle-mount on croup, facing left, left leg in front; pivot, circling left leg backward to straddle-mount in saddle, facing front.
8. Leap to same position, facing right, right leg in front; pivot, circling right leg backward to straddle-mount in saddle, facing front.

Fig. 24.

9. Back-shears-mount; twist body right or left and pivot forward to straddle-mount in saddle, facing rear.
10. Leap to straddle-mount on croup, facing left, right leg in front; pivot; left leg forward and face to the right; then right leg forward and face rear.
11. Same, from same mount, facing in the opposite direction.

APPARATUS. 233

SIXTH SERIES.

Free-rest.

FIG. 25.

In the free-rest the legs are swung upward to the rear until the body is horizontal, arms extended.
1. Leap to free-rest, hands on croup, and dismount to take-off. Fig. 25.
2. Same, with hands in saddle, and straddle-mount, facing front.
3. Same, with mount on knees.
4. Same, with squatting-mount.
5. Same, with back-shears-mount.
6. Same, dropping to leaning-rest, and snap off backward.
7. Leap to free-rest, hands in saddle, and drop off to the right or left.

MANUAL OF PHYSICAL TRAINING.

Seventh Series.

Rear-vaults.

As a preliminary of these vaults, practice the leg circles. The men should be cautioned to keep the buttocks close to the horse, lean the weight back, well over the hand on the side of the vault, land keep the legs extended. Take-off is from both feet.

Fig. 26.

In the beginning the feet are raised waist high only; later they should be raised to the height of the chest, the head, and finally higher than the head.

1. Rear-vault right. Fig. 26.
2. Rear-vault left.
3. Same exercises, facing the horse, or about.

APPARATUS. 235

Flank-vaults.

The flank-vaults do not differ materially from those of the side horse, except that the hands are placed in a different position. In the flank-vaults to the right, the right hand is placed close to the

FIG. 27.

end of the croup, fingers turned toward the take-off; the left hand is thrown forward well over to the right of the croup, fingers turned in the direction of the vault.

4. Flank-vault right. Fig. 27.
5. Same, left.
6. Flank-vault right, facing rear.
7. Flank-vault left, facing rear.

236   MANUAL OF PHYSICAL TRAINING.

Eighth Series.
Front-vaults.

This is the most difficult of these vaults. The support is the same as for the flank-vaults.

1. Front-vault right. Fig. 28.

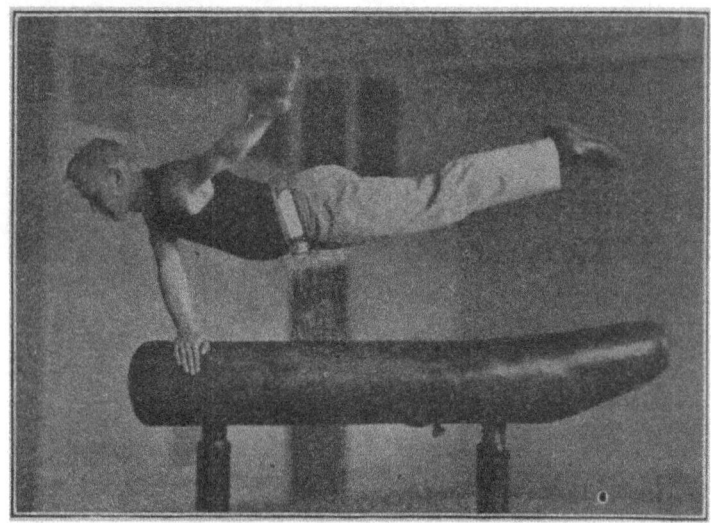

Fig. 28.

The movement begins on the left side, the legs being swung obliquely backward to the left first, and then the whole body, face down, extended as it is on the side horse, is pivoted on the right arm until it faces to the rear where the dismount takes place.

2. Same, left.
3. Front-vault right, with turn, facing horse.
4. Same, left.

APPARATUS.

Stride-vaults.

In these exercises one leg is circled over the croup and joined to the other leg before alighting. The circle is a horizontal one and must be executed with snap, else it will fail to catch up with the other leg, which has a shorter distance to cover. Legs must be extended.

5. Stride-vault with right leg (dismount on left side of horse, facing front.)
6. Same, with left leg.
7. Same, with the right, turning to the right and facing the horse.
8. Same, with the left.
9. Same, right or left, facing about.

NINTH SERIES.

Straddle-vaults.

In the following vaults the horse is cleared lengthwise. When the support is on the neck, the vault is more easily acquired if the legs are slightly beyond the horizontal in the rear when the hands land on the horse. This position drives the body forward; if the legs are below the horizontal, the weight is dragged back. The men must be cautioned not to throw the head back before the hands are released, because if they do a strained back is the result. Assistance should be given in these long jumps, and it is best rendered by a man standing close enough to catch hold of the arm of the one exercising, and yet not interfering unless his assistance is required. As a preliminary the men should be made to execute every exercise to the mount on the neck first.

1. Straddle-vault over horse, support on saddle and then on neck.
2. Straddle-vault, support one hand on saddle and the other on neck.
3. Same, with support on one hand on croup, the other on the neck.
4. Straddle-vault, support on neck, both hands forward as far as possible, fingers over end of horse. Fig. 29.

238 MANUAL OF PHYSICAL TRAINING.

FIG. 29.

HIGH HORIZONTAL BARS—HORIZONTAL VAULTING BARS.

HORIZONTAL BAR EXERCISES.

As the object of the following exercises is not the development of gymnastic proficiency, only such simple movements are prescribed that will develop and bring into play those muscle groups upon which a soldier must depend in successfully overcoming obstacles that may present themselves to him in the field.

The bar should be placed high enough to allow the soldier to hang in the extended-arm hang without touching the ground or floor with his toes. In the absence of a regular bar one may be improvised of two by four scantling, edges being rounded to permit a firm grip.

The grips used in these various exercises are:

(a) Ordinary grip; Knuckles turned to the rear, thumbs around bar.

(b) Reversed grip; Knuckles turned forward, thumbs around bar.

(c) Combined grip; A combination of the two.

FIRST SERIES.

1. Leap to extended-side-arm-hang—ordinary grip; LEAP. DROP.

    Assume the position of attention directly under the bar; at *Leap* spring upward, swing the arms forward and upward, grasping the bar with the ordinary grip and hang with arms extended. In this position the body is held as follows: Head erect; arms extended; distance between hands width of hips; back arched slightly; legs extended and closed; toes together and depressed. At *Drop* release the hands, swing the arms to the sides without bending them; light on toes, bending knees, and resume the position of attention smartly. Fig. 1.

240 MANUAL OF PHYSICAL TRAINING.

2. Repeat several times, assuming the position of attention each time.
3. Repeat several times, leaping back to the hang immediately after dropping.

FIG. 1.

4. Repeat 1, 2, and 3 with reversed grip.
5. Repeat 1, 2, and 3, hanging crosswise, right (left) hand in front.
6. Leap to extended-side-arm-hang, ordinary grip, at one side of bar, and travel sideward, hand after hand.
7. Same, traveling sideward, hand over hand.

HIGH HORIZONTAL BARS.

Second Series.

8. Same, traveling sideward, moving both hands simultaneously.
9. Repeat above exercises with reversed grip.
10. Repeat, in the cross-hang, traveling forward or backward.

Fig. 2.

11. Leap to extended-side-arm-hang, right hand ordinary and left hand in reversed grip; release right hand, turn right about on left arm, replace right hand in reversed grip, and turn left about on right arm; replace left hand in ordinary grip.
12. Leap to extended-side-arm-hang, ordinary grip, in middle of bar; change to stretch hang, moving first one and then the other hand outward; return to original position. Fig. 2.

MANUAL OF PHYSICAL TRAINING.

Third Series.

1. Leap to extended-side-arm-hang, ordinary grip; change right to reverse grip; then left; right back to ordinary grip; then left.
2. Same, from reversed grip to ordinary grip and back again.

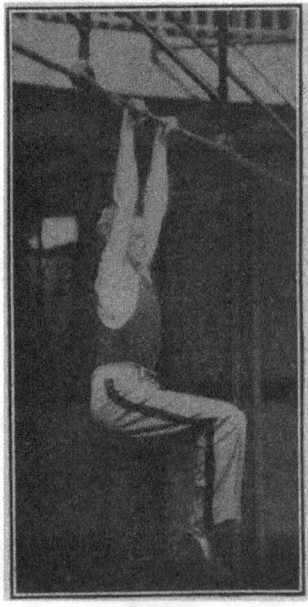

Fig. 3.

3. Leap as in 1; change right and then left hand to reversed grip; change both hands at same time to ordinary grip.
4. Leap to extended-side-arm-hang, reversed grip; change hand after hand to ordinary grip, and both back to reversed grip.
5. Leap to extended-side-arm-hang, ordinary grip; change both simultaneously to reversed grip, and back again to ordinary grip.

HIGH HORIZONTAL BARS. 243

The tendency in these exercises is to move the legs when the hands are being changed. This can be overcome if the body is drawn up slightly and the change made while the arms are slightly bent.

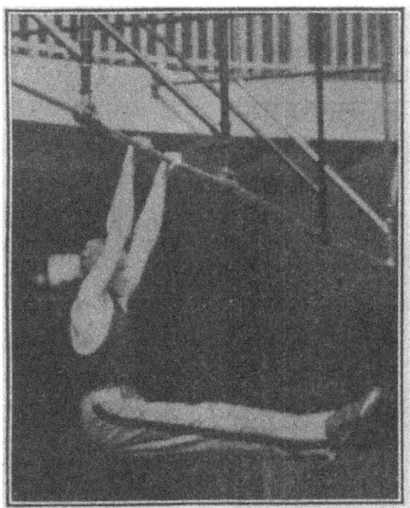

FIG. 4.

FOURTH SERIES.

6. Leap to extended-side-arm-hang, ordinary grip; raise and lower heel or heels; knees remain closed.
7. Same, raising knee or knees forward. Fig. 3.
8. Same, straddling and closing legs sideward.
9. Same, raising one leg forward horizontally.
10. Same, raising one knee and then extending leg forward.
11. Same as 10, with both legs. Fig. 4.

MANUAL OF PHYSICAL TRAINING.

Fifth Series.

1. Leap to extended-side-arm-hang, ordinary grip, and slightly bend and extend arms (rocking movement) alternately.
2. Leap as in 1, and draw body to bent-arm-hang, and drop from that position. Fig. 5.
3. Same as 2; extending arms and then dropping.
4. Leap to bent-arm-hang, ordinary grip, at once, and drop. Fig. 5.
5. Same, with reversed grip.

Fig. 5.

Fig. 6.

Sixth Series.

6. Leap to bent-knee-instep-balance-hang.

    To assume this position, leap to the bent-arm-hang with knees raised; pass knees between arms until insteps touch front of bar, at the same time extend the arms; lower legs and drop. Fig. 6.

HIGH HORIZONTAL BARS. 245

7. Execute 6 without pausing; also with reversed grip.
8. Leap to bent-knee-heel-balance-hang. This position is exactly like 6, except that the heels touch the rear of bar.

FIG. 7.

9. Leap to extended-side-arm-hang backward, i. e., execute 8; turn body through between arms and extend knees downward; release hands and drop. Fig. 7.
10. Same as 9, but return by drawing the legs back between the arms to extended-side-arm-hang forward and drop.

SEVENTH SERIES.

1. Leap to right-outer-knee-hang. Fig. 8.

   To assume this position, execute the bent-knee-instep-balance-hang (6, Sixth Series) first; then pass the right foot under and then over the bar outside of hand and rest leg on bar under knee, toes are extended and leg is horizontal; left leg is extended forward horizontally; arms extended. Return in reverse order and drop.

FIG. 8.

2. Leap to inner-knee-hang on right knee, leg between hands. Fig. 9.
3. Execute 1 and 2 with left leg.
4. Leap to inner-knee-hang on both knees, knees between hands. Fig. 10.
5. Leap to outer-knee-hang on both knees, knees outside of hand.

HIGH HORIZONTAL BARS. 247

FIG. 9.

FIG. 10.

248　　　　MANUAL OF PHYSICAL TRAINING.

EIGHTH SERIES.

1. Leap to outer-knee-hang (Fig. 8) and swing forward and backward.
2. Leap to inner-knee-hang; swing forward and backward.

Assume an outer or inner-knee-hang, and in that position swing backward and forward. The swing is gained by raising

FIG. 11.

the extended leg close to the bar and then forcing it downward, without bending it, as far as possible. Every time the body swings to the front this leg repeats the movement. To return to the extended-arm-hang, release the hanging knee just as the highest point of the forward swing is reached and join it to the other leg.

HIGH HORIZONTAL BARS. 249

3. Front-outer-knee-swing, to bent-arm and thigh-rest, Fig. 11; swing back to knee-hang; lower legs and drop.

In this exercise the arms draw the body toward the bar, and when sufficient swing has been gained the extended leg is forced down hard when the body is about to be raised upon the

FIG. 12.

bar. To return, the body is lowered slowly to the knee-hang and the hanging knee released.
4. Same as 3, extending arms from the bent to the extended-arm and thigh-rest on the bar. Fig. 12.
5. Same exercise, but swing up at once to the extended-rest.
6. Same as 3, 4, and 5, from inner-knee-hang.

MANUAL OF PHYSICAL TRAINING.

Ninth Series.

1. Leap to bent-arm-hang, hands reversed, with knees raised. Fig. 13.
2. Leap as above and immediately extend knees and front-circle-up-swing, Fig. 14, to bent-arm-rest on bar. Fig. 15.

    As the knees are extended the legs are thrown over the bar and the body is circled backward to the bent-arm-rest; and turn over to the hang.

FIG. 13.   FIG. 14.

3. Same, going from bent to extended-arm-rest, Fig. 16; bend arms and turn over.
4. Same, going to the extended-arm-rest at once.
5. Repeat, with the ordinary grip.
6. Repeat any of the above and lower body slowly to the bent and then to the extended-arm-hang.

HIGH HORIZONTAL BARS.

Fig. 15.

Fig. 16.

Tenth Series.

1. Leap to bent-arm-hang, ordinary grip, and raise right forearm over bar to elbow-hang on right arm; return to the extended-hang, and drop.
2. Same with the left arm.

FIG. 17.   FIG. 18.

3. Same, raising first the right and then the left forearm to elbow-hang on both arms; change to the extended-hang, moving both arms simultaneously. Fig. 17.
4. Same, moving both arms over the bar at once.
5. Pull the body up from the extended to the bent-arm-hang and repeat from 1 to 4.
6. From the arm-hang, Fig. 17, raise the right elbow and then the left elbow to the bent-arm-rest, Fig. 15, and extend both arms to the extended-arm-rest, Fig. 16. Fig. 18.

HORIZONTAL VAULTING BAR.

For beginners and for general use the bar should be about 3 feet 6 inches high; later proficiency should determine the height.

First Lesson.

1. Leap to extended-arm-rest, ordinary grip. Fig. 16.
    While in the extended-arm-rest execute:
2. Raising and lowering heel or heel.
3. Straddle and close legs sideward.
4. Raise leg backward horizontally.
5. Same sideward.
6. Travel sideward, right (left), hand after hand.

Second Lesson.

1. Leap to back-extended-arm-rest. Fig. 19.
    Right hand grasps bar opposite left shoulder; in leaping, face left about and grasp bar with left hand.
2. Same, facing right about.
3. In the back-rest, execute the various leg exercises. Dismount by dropping off or by swinging off.
    The dismount or drop from the above exercise may be the ordinary drop from the rest; from the rest with legs or body in any of the positions described above; or the body may be swung off backward.
4. Leap and raise leg over bar to outer-thigh-mount, knee bent.
5. Same, with knee extended. Fig. 20.
6. Inner-thigh-mount, leg bent; leg passes under hand.
7. Same, with leg extended. Fig. 21.

Fig. 19.

HIGH HORIZONTAL BARS. 255

Fig. 20.

Fig. 21.

Third Lesson.

1. Circle right leg inward, under right hand, to thigh-mount, Fig. 21, facing front; leg is extended downward; return to the stand by circling the leg back under right hand.
2. Same with the left leg.
3. Same as 1 and 2, but circling the leg backward under opposite hand to the stand.
4. Circle right leg outward, under the left hand, to the thigh-mount as in 1, and dismount by swinging the leg backward under the opposite hand or the hand on the same side.
5. Circle right leg inward as in 1; pause in the mount only momentarily and complete circle under left hand.
6. Same with left leg.
7. Circle right leg outward as in 4; pause in the mount momentarily and complete circle under right hand.

Fourth Lesson.

1. Circle right leg forward, under right or left hand, to inner-thigh-mount, knee bent; reverse right hand and dismount on opposite side of bar, facing to the right, by raising the left leg forward. Fig. 22.
2. Same, with the left leg.
3. Circle right leg and then left leg forward to the back-rest and drop or swing off forward.
4. Same as 3, from the back-rest the legs are circled backward again to the front-rest; drop or swing off backward.
5. Leap to back-rest Fig. 19, and circle legs backward to front-rest and forward to back-rest.
6. Circle right leg forward, under right or left hand; face about and circle left leg backward to the stand.
7. Same, with the left leg.

Fig. 22.

Fifth Lesson.

1. Leap to extended-arm-rest, right hand reversed, and swing legs over bar on left to the stand, facing right.
2. Same on the opposite side.
3. Flank-vault right. (*See* Side horse.)
4. Same on the left.
5. Rear-vault on the right. (*See* Side horse.)
6. Same on the left.
7. Front-vault on the right. (*See* Side horse.)
8. Same on the left.

Sixth Lesson.

1. Squatting-vault, releasing right hand.
2. Same, releasing left hand.
3. Squatting-vault, releasing both hands.
4. Flank-vault right, with ¼ turn left.
5. Same on opposite side.
6. Rear-vault on the right, with ¼ turn right.
7. Same on opposite side.
8. Front-vault on the right, with ¼ turn left.
9. Same on opposite side.

Seventh Lesson.

1. Squatting-vault, with ¼ turn right or left.
2. Same, with ½ turn.
3. Rear-vault right, facing bar, and squatting vault.
4. Same, left.
5. Rear-vault as in 3, right or left, and flank-vault right or left.
6. Rear-vault as in 3, right or left, and front-vault right or left.
7. Rear-vault as in 3, right or left, and rear-vault right or left.
8. Squatting-vault as in 2, and rear, flank, or front-vault.

PARALLEL BARS.

In the following series all movements of a slow and cumbersome nature, the so-called strength exercises, and those in which considerable continued strain is thrown upon the upper back, chest and arm muscles, have been eliminated; instead, only such that make for activity and agility and in which the support of the body upon the arms is only momentary are prescribed. In many respects these exercises are very similar to those on the horses and vaulting bars, and, like these, their greatest value lies in quick and speedy execution. All of the prescribed exercises are well within the capabilities of men of ordinary strength.

The series should first be practiced on bars 4 feet high, the height being gradually increased to 5 feet as the proficiency of the men increases. The width of the bars should equal the width of the shoulders of the average man of the squad.

FIRST SERIES.

ARM-REST AND EXERCISES IN THE REST.

1. To the extended cross-arm-rest—1. Ready, 2. LEAP, 3. DROP.

    The position of attention is assumed at arm's length from the ends of the bars. At *Ready* the arms are raised forward between the bars and the hands are placed upon the ends of the bars, knuckles turned inward slightly, and the body is raised on toes. At *Leap* spring upward into the rest. In that position the head is erect, shoulders square, chest out, arms extended, back arched slightly, legs straight and closed, toes together and depressed. At *Drop* the body is permitted to drop back to the take-off without bending arms, hands being turned in slightly, light on toes, bend knees slightly,

260   MANUAL OF PHYSICAL TRAINING.

and as these are extending drop arms to the sides smartly and
resume the position of attention.   Fig. 1.
2. Repeat above exercise several times.
3. Repeat, going back to the rest without resuming the position of
attention.

FIG. 1.

In the extended-arm-rest:
4. Raise and lower heel or heels.
5. Raise and lower knee or knees.   Fig. 2.
6. Side or cross straddle legs.

PARALLEL BARS.

FIG. 2.

MANUAL OF PHYSICAL TRAINING.

Second Series.

1. Raise knee and extend leg forward. Fig. 3.
2. Turn body right or left.
3. Turn body right and then left about.

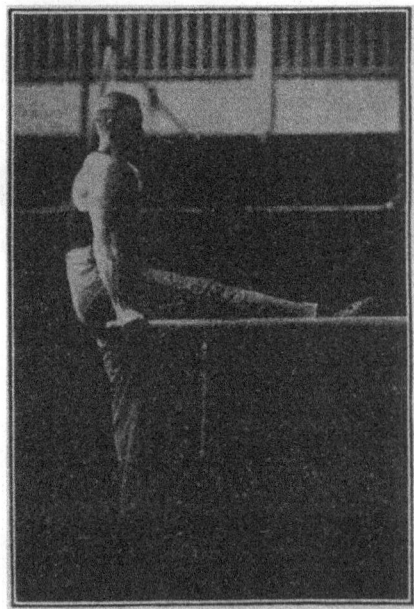

Fig. 3.

4. Raise hands alternately, marking time.
5. Move right hand forward, three movements, to stretch-rest, and back again. Same, left. Fig. 4.
6. Travel forward, hands alternating, three to five movements, and drop between bars, facing right or left.

PARALLEL BARS.

FIG. 4.

264   MANUAL OF PHYSICAL TRAINING.

Third Series.

From the stand to the stand:
1. Straddle-mount on both bars. Fig. 5.

    Knees are extended, toes depressed, trunk and head erect, arms straight, and legs almost at right angles to the body.

Fig. 5.

2. Straddle-mount on one bar. Fig. 6.
    Legs are closed under the bar.
3. Oblique-mount on right or left bar. Legs closed. Fig. 7.
4. Side-mount on right or left bar, facing right or left. Fig. 8.

PARALLEL BARS. 265

5. Change from one of the various mounts to any other.

   In these changes the legs are swung up and then in the direction of the mount.

FIG. 6.

6. Leap to the extended-arm-rest and from there execute the various mounts, going back to the rest before dropping back to the take-off.

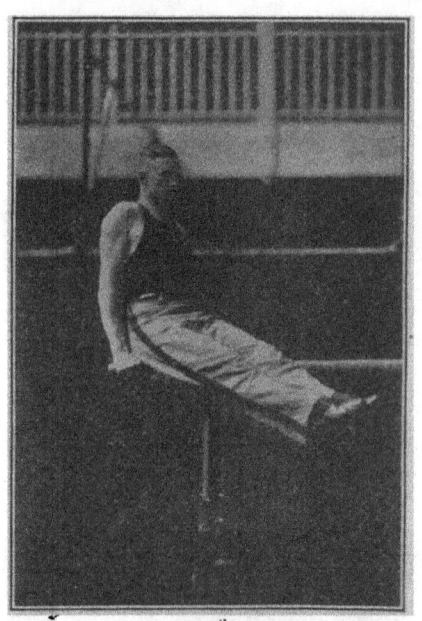

Fig. 7.

PARALLEL BARS.

FIG. 8.

Fourth Series.

1. Straddle-mount on both bars; change hands forward and swing legs forward to the straddle-mount; repeat to end of bars and drop off, facing right or left.
2. Change forward in the same manner from the straddle-mount on one bar; from the oblique or from the side-mount.
3. Oblique-mount on right bar; change hands to left bar, and circle right leg forward to straddle-mount, facing rear; snap-off forward right. Fig. 9.

    In the snap-off both legs are swung up and then moved in the direction indicated.
4. Oblique-mount on right bar; change hands to left and circle right leg over right bar, then between bars and then forward to straddle-mount on both bars; snap-off right or left.
5. Oblique-mount on right bar; face left about to oblique-mount on same bar, facing rear; circle left leg forward to straddle-mount, facing take-off, hands in front of body, and dismount to take-off.
6. Oblique-mount on right bar, circle right leg forward to straddle mount on both bars, facing left, right knee bent; pivot left leg forward to straddle-mount on both bars, facing rear, and snap-off.
7. Oblique-mount on left bar; circle left leg forward as in 6.

    The hand upon which the weight rests is always upon the bar opposite to the one upon which the supporting thigh rests.

PARALLEL BARS.

Fig. 9.

Fifth Series.

1. Straddle-mount on both bars, and snap-off right or left without or with turns.
2. Same from straddle-mounts on one bar, snapping off over opposite bar.
3. Same from oblique-mounts.
4. Same from side-mounts.
5. Straddle-mount on both bars; change hands forward and snap-off backward without or with turns.
6. Same from straddle-mount on one bar, on the same or opposite side.
7. Same as 6 from oblique-mounts.
8. Same as 7 from side-mounts.

Sixth Series.

1. Straddle-mount on both bars; change hands forward; swing legs forward; vault forward without turning. Fig. 10.
2. Same, from the straddle-mounts on one bar, the oblique-mounts, or side-mounts.
3. Straddle-mount on both bars; change hands forward and swing legs forward and backward, and vault backward, right or left.
4. Same from the various other mounts.
5. Execute 1 and 2 with quarter or half turn toward bars.
6. Execute 3 and 4 with quarter or half turn away from bars.

PARALLEL BARS.

Fig. 10.

Seventh Series.

1. Oblique-mount right or left; change to the front-leaning-rest, and dismount backward right or left. Fig. 11.

    From the oblique-mount on the right bar the right foot is placed on the left bar and the body is turned. The left foot is placed on the right bar, the hands are on the ends of the bars, facing the take-off. In this position the arms and legs are extended, shoulders well over hands; the feet rest on the inside of the instep. To dismount, drop off to the right or left.

2. Straddle-mount on both bars; change hands forward, and swing forward to straddle-mount; change to front-leaning-rest by swinging backward, and dismount backward right or left.

3. Stand between bars; leap to extended-arm-rest in middle, and swing backward to front-leaning-rest.

    Having assumed the front-leaning-rest by means of one of the various methods described above, execute the following exercises:

4. Bend and extend arms. Fig. 12.
5. Draw legs to squatting-position and extend again. Fig. 13.
6. Place both hands on one and both feet on the other bar. Fig. 14.
7. Bend arms and lower elbows, resting on upper arms. To recover, raise first one elbow and then the other. Fig. 15.
8. Same as 7, recover by raising both elbows simultaneously.

PARALLEL BARS.

Fig. 11.

274   MANUAL OF PHYSICAL TRAINING.

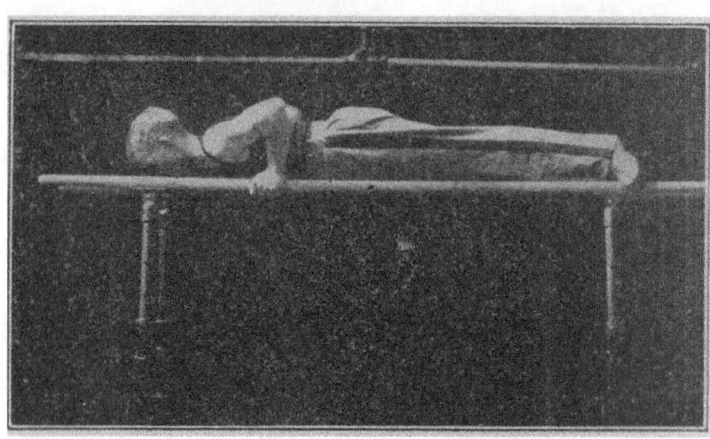

FIG. 12.

FIG. 13.

PARALLEL BARS.

Fig. 14.

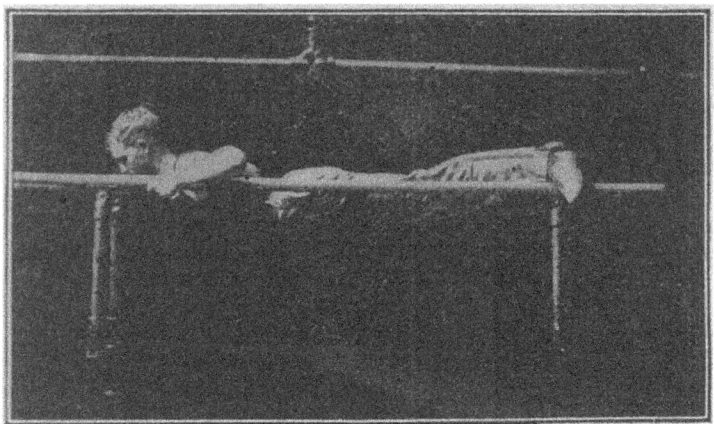

Fig. 15.

Eighth Series.

1. Straddle-mount on both bars; change to back-leaning-rest; change to straddle-mount, and snap-off. Fig. 16.

   The feet, outside of insteps touching, are placed on the bars and the body is raised until the back is well arched; arms remain extended.

Fig. 16.

2. Swing to the back-leaning-rest from the straddle-mount, hands forward, at the end or in the middle of bars.

   In that position execute the following exercises:
3. Bend and extend body. Figs. 17 and 16.
4. Swing from back to front-leaning-rest and reverse.
5. Vault backward right or left with swings, from the leaning-rests.

PARALLEL BARS.

Fig. 17.

Ninth Series.

Position in the middle; bars shoulder high.
1. Leap to upper-arm-hang and drop between bars. Fig. 18.

    In that position the arms, elbows slightly bent, are thrown over the bars, hands grasping the bars firmly; legs are closed, toes depressed; back is arched slightly; shoulders square and head erect. In dismounting the hands are turned inward and the arms are dropped smartly as the knees are extending.

    In that position execute:
2. Various leg exercises.
3. Swing legs backward and forward, dismounting at the end of rear swing.
4. Swing as in 3 to back-thigh and arm-rest. Fig. 19.

    Legs are straddled over bars in forward swing, body and legs extended; swing legs backward and dismount at end of rear swing, between bars.
5. Same, to front-thigh and arm-rest. Fig. 20.

    Legs are straddled over bars in rear swing; close legs and dismount between bars.
6. Same in rear and front swing.

PARALLEL BARS.

Fig. 18.

280 MANUAL OF PHYSICAL TRAINING.

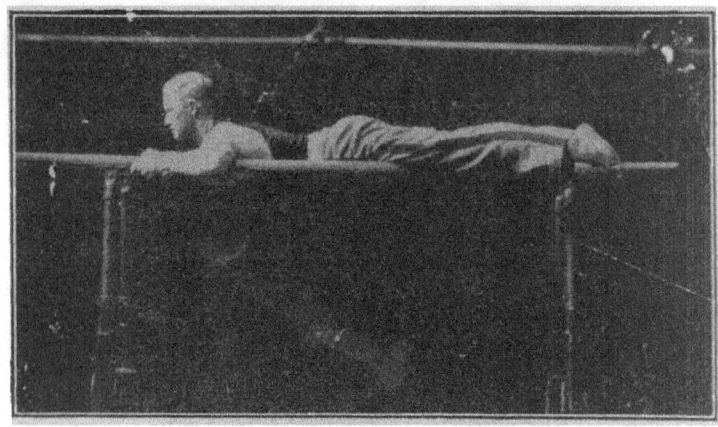

FIG. 19.

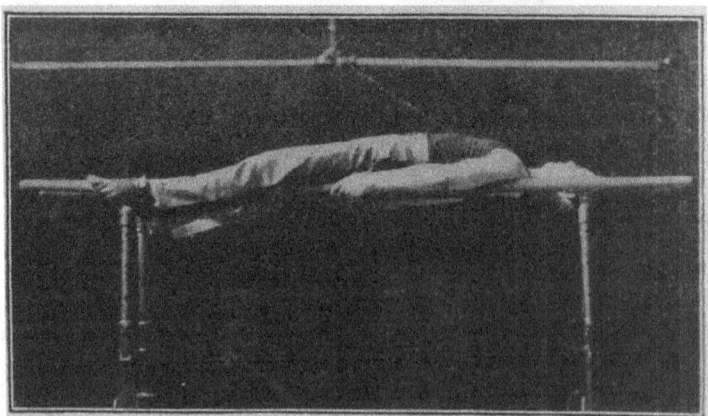

FIG. 20.

PARALLEL BARS.

Tenth Series.

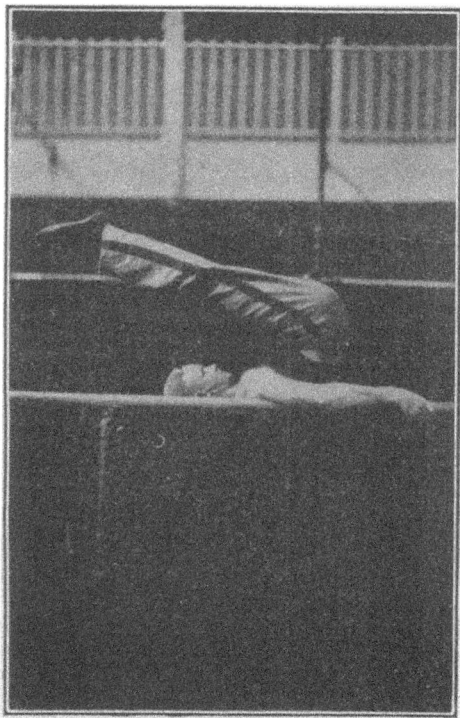

Fig. 21.

1. Swing as in 3 to overhead-balance. Fig. 21.

    Legs are swung over head until head and knees are close together and a balance may be maintained without much effort.

2. Swing to back-thigh and arm-rest; Fig. 19, change to straddle-mount on the bars and snap or vault off.
3. Swing to front-thigh and arm-rest; Fig. 20, draw legs forward to straddle-mount and snap or vault off.

FIG. 22.

4. Execute 1 and roll to straddle-mount in front of hands and snap or vault off.
5. Swing and raise body to straddle-mount at end of rear swing. Snap or vault off.
6. Upper-arm-hang, draw body forward to hands; raise right elbow, then left and extend arms to extended-arm-rest, and drop backward between bars. Fig. 22.

PARALLEL BARS.

ELEVENTH SERIES.

The following exercises will be executed from the take-off, and the dismount will be back to the take-off. Height of bars, 4 feet.
1. Leap to momentary rest on hands and circle right leg backward under right hand to the take-off.
2. Same with left leg.
3. Same with right and follow immediately with the left leg.
4. Leap and circle right leg forward over end of bar under right hand to momentary rest and drop to take-off.
5. Same with left leg.
6. Same with right and follow immediately with the left leg.

TWELFTH SERIES.

1. Circle right leg forward; drop to take-off, and circle left backward.
2. Same forward left or backward right.
3. Same as 1 and 2 in reverse order, i. e., right backward and left forward; left backward and right forward.
4. Circle right leg forward over right bar to the oblique-mount on the left bar; snap-off.

    In this exercise both legs are moved forward simultaneously, the right on the outside of the bars, the right outside of the right bar and the left between the bars. The body is inclined to the left and the weight is entirely on the left arm immediately after the feet leave the take-off.
5. Same with the left leg to the oblique-mount on the right bar.
6. Leap and straddle both legs over ends of bars to the straddle-mount behind the hands; change hands and snap-off right or left.

    As the feet leave the take-off the legs are separated and the arms thrust the body up and forward; the hands moving forward; when the mount is completed the hands are changed to the rear.
7. Same as 6, decreasing the interval between changes of hands and the mount and dismount as much as possible.

THIRTEENTH SERIES.

From the stand on the take-off:
1. Vault forward right.
2. Same to the left.
3. Same right and left to the stand, facing the bars.
4. Same to the right and left; to the stand, facing away from bars.
5. Vault forward right to stand, facing left about.
6. Same to the left, facing right about.
7. Same to the right, facing right about.
8. Same to the left, facing left about.

FOURTEENTH SERIES.

Repeat the vaults prescribed in the thirteenth series with a running start of about 6 paces; the take-off is moved about a foot from the ends of the bars and the jump is from both feet; the support is on the ends of the bars.

FIFTEENTH SERIES.

Repeat the thirteenth series with a running start as in the fourteenth series, the support being in the middle of the bars.

In leaping from the take-off the arms must be swung forward and upward between the bars, not over them. Fig. 23.
1. Leap to straddle-mount in middle of bars behind hands; change hands behind body and swing backward and vault backward over right bar. Fig. 24.
2. Same, left.
3. Same, right or left to stand, facing bar.
4. Leap to extended-arm-rest in middle of bars and swing backward and vault backward as in 1.
5. Same to the left.
6. Same to the right or left to stand, facing bars.

PARALLEL BARS. 285

Sixteenth Series.

From the stand on the take-off:
1. Repeat 4 and 5 of the Twelfth Series, to the right and left.
2. Circle left leg forward over left bar, and vault forward to the right.

Fig. 23.

The left leg is swung forward over the left bar and the right leg between the bars, and both legs then passing over the right bar to stand, facing to the front. The body must be sharply inclined to the right and the support must be on the right arm the moment the feet leave the take-off.
3. Same to the left.
4. Same to the right, facing the bar.
5. Same to the left, facing the bar.

286 MANUAL OF PHYSICAL TRAINING.

FIG. 24.

RINGS.

Rings should be hung on adjustable straps, which will allow them to be used at any height, from height of chest to jumping height. Circular rings whose inside diameter is about 7 inches—outside an inch and a quarter more—are the best for all purposes.

EXERCISES ON RINGS AT HEIGHT OF CHEST.

First Series.

In all ring exercises the hands grasp the rings with knuckles turned out, the side of the rings being parallel to the sides of the body.

From the stand between the rings:
1. Lower body to back-extended-arm-leaning-hang. Fig. 1.
2. Lower body to front-extended-arm-leaning-hang. Fig. 2.
3. Lower as in 2; and from there to position 1.
4. Lower to side-extended-arm-leaning-hang, right or left. Fig. 3.
5. Change from right side-leaning-hang to the same position on the left.
6. From back-extended-leaning-hang continue to circle body right or left.

288 MANUAL OF PHYSICAL TRAINING.

FIG. 1.

Fig. 2.

290   MANUAL OF PHYSICAL TRAINING.

FIG. 3.

RINGS. 291

Second Series.

FIG. 4.

1. From the stand between rings, leap and turn over backward to the back-stand, and forward again to original position.
2. Raise knee or leg forward.
3. Bend and extend arms.
4. Turn body right or left.
5. Bend body at waist and extend.
6. Leap to the inverted-hang. Fig. 4.
    Legs between ropes, head down.

Third Series.

FIG. 5.

1. Inverted-hang; slightly bend and extend arms, feet against ropes.
2. Leap to nest-hang. Fig. 5.
    Insert feet in rings and turn body through until back is well arched.
3. Leap to right (left) knee-hang. Fig. 6.
    Right leg is thrown over right arm, knee bent; left leg is extended forward horizontally.

FIG. 6.

4. Leap to right (left) knee-hang and swing extended leg forward and back.
5. Leap to extended-leg-balance. Fig. 7.
6. Leap to bent-knee-hang-leg-balance. Fig. 8.

294 MANUAL OF PHYSICAL TRAINING.

Fig. 7.

RINGS.

FIG. 8.

296   MANUAL OF PHYSICAL TRAINING.

Fourth Series.

From the extended-leg-balance, 6, execute:
1. Change to inverted-hang; to nest-hang; to knee-hang; to hammock-hang, etc.
2. Leap to rest on hands and dismount.   Fig. 9.

FIG. 9.

3. Various leg exercises in the rest.
4. Swing legs forward and backward in the rest.
5. Swing legs in the bent-arm-rest and turn over backward to the stand.
6. From extended-arm-rest bend to the bent-arm-rest and return to extended-arm-rest.

RINGS.

Exercises on Rings at Height of Reach.

Fifth Series.

The rings should be adjusted so as to admit of a spring from the floor.

1. Leap to bent or extended-leg-balance-hang.
2. Leap and turn over backward to back-hang, and drop from there.
3. Same, and return to stand.
4. Leap to balance-hang, 1, and extend to inverted-hang, legs between ropes.
5. Leap as in 4; return to balance-hang; then to back-hang, and drop to stand.
6. Leap to nest-hang.
7. Leap to bent-arm-hang.   Fig. 10.

Sixth Series.

1. From 7 swing legs backward and forward.
2. Same, bending knees in forward and raising heels in backward swing.
3. Swing legs to leg balance.
4. Swing legs to nest-hangs.
5. Swing legs to knee-hangs.
6. Swing legs to inverted-hang.
7. Swing legs and turn-over backward to back-hang, and drop.

298 MANUAL OF PHYSICAL TRAINING.

FIG. 10.

RINGS. 299

EXERCISES ON RINGS AT JUMPING HEIGHT.

1. Leap to extended-arm-hang and execute various leg exercises. Fig. 11.

FIG. 11.

2. Swing legs forward and backward, waist high; drop to the stand at end of rear swing.
3. Same, swinging legs to height of shoulders, head, or over head.
4. Swing legs forward and backward, and turn-over backward to back-hang, and drop to the stand.
5. Same, returning from back-hang to front-hang.

6. Swing legs forward and backward, keeping trunk in upright position as much as possible.
7. Circle-swing legs right or left.

   The legs are swung around in a circle without twisting the arms or body.

Eighth Series.

1. Swing legs forward and backward and slightly bend arms at end of each swing.
2. Same, jerking rings at end of every swing.
3. Same, drawing body to bent-arm-hang at end of every forward swing, extending immediately so as not to break the swing.
4. Swing legs to extended-leg-balance and change to inverted-hang.
5. Same, to leg-balance and then turning over to back-hang, and returning to original position.
6. Swing legs to nest-hang.

GYMNASTIC CONTESTS.

These exercises are those in which the benefits are lost sight of in the pleasure their attainment provides, which in the case of these contests is the vanquishing of an opponent. The men are pitted against each other in pairs; age, height, weight, and general physical aptitude being the determining factors in the selection.

In the contests in which superiority is dependent upon skill and agility no restrictions need be placed upon the efforts of the contestants; but in those that are a test of strength and endurance it is well to call a contest a "draw", when the men are equally matched and the contest is likely to be drawn out to the point of exhaustion of one or both contestants.

It is recommended that these contests be indulged in once or twice a month and then at the conclusion of the regular drill.

Contests that require skill and agility should alternate with those that depend upon strength and endurance. In order to facilitate the instruction a number of pairs should be engaged at the same time.

1. Cane wrestling: The cane to be about an inch in diameter and a yard long, ends rounded. It is grasped with the right hand at the end, knuckles down, and with the left hand, knuckles up, inside of and close to the opponent's right hand. Endeavor is then made to wrest the cane from the opponent. Loss of grip with either hand loses the bout. Fig. 1.

2. Cane twisting: Same cane as in 1. Contestants grasp it as in 1, only the knuckles of both hands are up, and the arms are extended overhead. Object: The contestants endeavor to make the cane revolve in their opponent's hands without allowing it to do so in their own. The cane must be forced down.

3. Cane pulling: Contestants sit on the ground, facing each other, legs straight and the soles of the feet in contact. The cane is grasped as in 2 but close to the feet. Object: To pull the opponent to his feet. The legs throughout the contest must be kept rigid. Fig. 2.

4. "Bucked" contest: Contestants sit on the ground "bucked"; i. e., the cane is passed under the knees, which are drawn up, and the arms passed under the cane with the fingers laced in front of the ankles. Object: To get the toes under those of the opponent and roll him over. Fig. 3.

5. Single pole pushing: Contestants grasp end of pole, 6 feet long and 2 inches thick, and brace themselves. Object: To push the opponent out of position. Fig. 4.

6. Double pole pushing: The poles are placed under the arms close to the arm pits, ends projecting. Object: Same as in 5. Fig. 5.

7. Double pole pulling: Position as in 6 but standing back to back. Object: To pull the opponent out of position. Fig. 6.

8. "Cock fight:" Contestants hop on one leg with the arms folded closely over the chest. Object: By butting with the fleshy part of the shoulder without raising the arms, or by dodging to make the opponent change his feet or touch the floor with his hand or other part of his body.

9. One-legged tug of war: Contestants hop on one leg and grasp hands firmly. Object: To pull the opponent forward or make him place the raised foot on the floor.

10. The "siege:" One contestant stands with one foot in a circle 14 inches in diameter, the other foot outside, and the arms folded as in 8. Two other contestants, each hopping on one leg, endeavor to dislodge the one in the circle by butting him with the shoulder. The besieged one is defeated in case he raises the foot in the circle, or removes it entirely from the circle. The besiegers are defeated in case they change feet or touch the floor as in 8. As soon as either of the latter is defeated his place is immediately filled, so that there

GYMNASTIC CONTESTS.

Fig. 1.

Fig. 2.

304　　MANUAL OF PHYSICAL TRAINING.

Fig. 3.

Fig. 4.

GYMNASTIC CONTESTS.

Fig. 5.

Fig. 6.

are always two attacking. The besieged should resort to volting, ducking, etc., rather than to depend upon his strength.

11. One-armed tug: Contestants stand facing each other; right hands grasped, feet apart. Object: Without moving feet, to pull the opponent forward. Shifting the feet loses the bout. Fig. 7.

12. "Tug royal:" Three contestants stand facing inward and grasp each others wrists securely and with their feet outside a circle about three feet in diameter. Object: By pulling or pushing to make one of the contestants step inside of the circle.

13. Indian wrestling: Contestants lie upon the ground face up, right shoulders in close contact, right elbows locked; at *one* the right leg is raised overhead and lowered, this is repeated at *two*, and at *three* the leg is raised quickly and locked with the opponent's right leg. Object: To roll him over by forcing his leg down. Fig. 8.

14. Medicine ball race: Teams of five or six men are organized and a track for each team is marked out. This track consists of marks on the floor or ground at distances of 4 yards. On each of these marks stands a man with legs apart, the team forming a column of files. At *ready, get set*, the contestants prepare for the race, and at *go* the first man in the column rolls a medicine ball, which he has on the floor in front of him, through his legs to No. 2, he in turn rolls it to 3, etc., when it reaches the last man he picks it up and runs to the starting place with it and, the others all having shifted back one mark, the rolling is repeated. This continues until the first man brings the ball back to the starting place and every man is in his original position. The ball should be kept rolling; each man, as it comes ot him, pushing it on quickly. Any ball about 9 inches in diameter will answer; it may be made of strong cloth and stuffed with cotton waste.

GYMNASTIC CONTESTS.

FIG. 7.

FIG. 8.

ATHLETICS.

The value of athletic training in the service is dependent upon the effect it has upon the mass, and not upon the effect it has upon the individual few. The training, in order to meet the requirements of the service, should have nothing in common with competitive athletics, but should be broad enough in the method of its application to reach out and include the development of every man to the extent of his capabilities in those branches of athletics the utility of which to the service is unquestioned. In other words, it should have an applicable value, be educational, and not spectacular, for it is the ability of the average of the mass that determines the efficiency of a fighting machine. Consequently it should be the aim of instructors to place this phase of the training of the men upon precisely the same plane as that of other portions of the soldier's education.

To attain this, it is necessary to eliminate those athletic events that have nothing to commend them from a military point of view, such as short-distance runs, pole vaulting, and hammer throwing. These events should be confined to the more skillful, for whose benefit an annual field day competition should be arranged. To the service the long distance, the half mile, mile, two and five mile runs, and the jumps are much more essential than the dashes, pole vaulting, etc.

This training should be conducted entirely out of doors, and in mapping out programs for the outdoor period instructors should alternate this work with the setting-up exercises, gymnastic contests and gymnastic games.

In order to stimulate interest, the men should be grouped into classes upon the basis of ability and promoted or demoted as their progress, or lack of it, warrants.

Instructors are cautioned to go about this training cautiously and train the men carefully; by doing so they will not fail to obtain good results and avoid those injuries that are directly chargeable to over-indulgence and over-exertion. In the following progressive method squads of from 10 to 12 men may be trained at the same time, each squad under the supervision of a non-commissioned officer or trained enlisted man, and all under the direction of the athletic officer.

A distinction is made between *double timing, running*, and the flexion run.

Double timing has for its purpose the quick advancement of troops in the shortest space of time with the least expenditure of physical effort, commensurate with military traditions which still demand that the carriage of the body should assume a certain uniform attitude during this method of progression. In double timing the saving in physical effort is made by diminishing the leg motions, thereby reducing the height of the flight of the body between the strides when neither foot is upon the ground and by curtailing the height the foot is raised.

Running is the most expensive, as well as the swiftest, method of progression the body is capable of, and differs from the double timing by the increased number and exaggerated character of the leg motions; by the increased force with which the body is thrust forward and upward by these motions, and by the increased demand upon the muscles of the trunk and neck, which are contracted in order to give the trunk and head that immobility without which speed is impossible. It is chiefly because of this immobility, which interferes seriously with respiration and which in turn affects the heart action, that running is so exhaustive. Thus, while running will develop lung, heart, and leg power, and endurance as no other form of exercise will, it does it with the ever-present liability to injury when carried to excess. Instructors are therefore cautioned to exercise the utmost care in its application, especially when handling untrained men.

Flexion run.—In this method of progression physical exertion is reduced to a minimum. The number of strides per minute is the same as in double timing, but a considerable latitude in the carriage of the body is permitted. As its name implies, the muscles of the entire body are flexed, relaxed as much as possible, and every movement is shorn of every unnecessary exaggeration. The trunk rests loosely upon the hips and is allowed to fall forward until the center of gravity falls on a point about the length of a stride in front of the body; the muscles of the shoulders, chest, and back are relaxed and the arms, flexed at the elbows, hang loosely by the sides; the knees are slightly flexed constantly and should never be fully extended; the feet are raised only high enough to clear the ground and are allowed to swing forward with the soles as nearly parallel to the ground as possible; in striking the ground the heels come in contact with it first, the toes, however, being raised only just high enough to keep them from becoming chafed by rubbing against the front of the shoes.

When properly assumed, the attitude of the body is such that the weight is constantly falling forward and the legs are moved forward in the effort to establish an ever changing equilibrum. This means of progression has been variously designated as the "dog trot," "running walk," and "fox gait," and is similar to the gait used by Indian runners and the jinrickisha men.

The advantages of this gait over all others lies in the fact that it produces the maximum results through the minimum of exertion; that the strain on the vital organs is reduced so that it is a little more than that caused by marching in quick time; and that, finally, it is dependent upon a greatly reduced muscular effort and not upon excessive respiratory, circulatory, or neural effort. When it becomes necessary to move troops rapidly it is almost imperative that they should reach their designation in such physical condition that they may be engaged actively with some assurance of success; therefore the value of this method to the service can hardly be overestimated.

In the following schedule the rate of the walk at increased gait is 140; that of the double timing and the flexion runs, 180; and that of the running, 220 steps per minute.

In the following schedule the men should be advanced only when they can cover the preceding distance without becoming exhausted or fatigued.

SCHEDULE.

1. ⅛ mile walk at increased gait, ⅛ mile flexion run, ⅛ mile walk.
2. ⅛ mile walk at increased gait, ¼ mile flexion run, ⅛ mile walk.
3. ⅛ mile walk at increased gait, ⅜ mile flexion run, ⅛ mile walk.
4. ⅛ mile walk at increased gait, ½ mile flexion run, ⅛ mile walk.
5. ⅛ mile walk at increased gait, ⅝ mile flexion run, ⅛ mile walk.
6. ⅛ mile walk at increased gait, ¾ mile flexion run, ⅛ mile walk.
7. ⅛ mile walk at increased gait, ⅞ mile flexion run, ⅛ mile walk.
8. ⅛ mile walk at increased gait, 1 mile flexion run, ⅛ mile walk.
9. ⅛ mile double timing, ½ mile flexion run, ⅛ mile walk.
10. ¼ mile double timing, ½ mile flexion run, ⅛ mile walk.
11. ¼ mile double timing, ⅝ mile flexion run, ⅛ mile walk.
12. ¼ mile double timing, ¾ mile flexion run, ⅛ mile walk.
13. ⅛ mile running, ½ mile flexion run, ⅛ mile walk.
14. ¼ mile running, ½ mile flexion run, ⅛ mile walk.
15. ¼ mile running, ⅝ mile flexion run, ⅛ mile walk.
16. ¼ mile running, ¾ mile flexion run, ⅛ mile walk.
17. ¼ mile running, ⅞ mile flexion run, ⅛ mile walk.
18. ¼ mile running, 1 mile flexion run, ⅛ mile walk.
19. ¼ mile running, 1⅛ miles flexion run, ⅛ mile walk.
20. ¼ mile running, 1¼ miles flexion run, ⅛ mile walk.
21. ¼ mile running, 1⅜ miles flexion run, ⅛ mile walk.
22. ¼ mile running, 1½ miles flexion run, ⅛ mile walk.

ATHLETICS.

23. ¼ mile running, 1⅝ miles flexion run, ⅛ mile walk.
24. 2 miles flexion run, ⅛ mile walk.
25. 2 miles double timing, ⅛ mile walk.
26. 1 mile running, 1 mile flexion run, ⅛ mile walk.

When the men become seasoned the above exercises should be practiced with light equipment, rifle, cartridge belt, and ammunition. The course may also be laid across country. A practical test approximating service conditions consists in having an entire organization cover the 2-mile course across country, equipped with rifle, belt, etc., the finish being the target range, where the men should immediately be engaged in a skirmish run.

JUMPING.

The following jumps should be first practiced to teach the men proper form, and when they have acquired this the jump should be for distance and height, or for a combination of the two.

1. Standing broad.
2. Standing high.
3. Standing broad-high.
4. Running broad.
5. Running high.
6. Running broad-high.
7. Standing three jumps.
8. Standing hop, step, and jump.
9. Running hop, step, and jump.

Whenever it is possible the obstacles to be cleared should be natural ones, such as would confront men in the field.

SWIMMING.

1. Arrangements for the instruction in swimming must be determined by the facilities existing at the various posts or stations.

At such of the latter where there is sufficient depth of water and available docks, swimming platforms can be readily erected. These platforms, which may be built in sections so that they can be removed after the swimming season, should project not less than 4 feet beyond the edge of the dock, and the distance from the platform floor to the surface of the water should not be less than 30 inches. The length of the platform will depend upon the available space and the number of men to be instructed. A space of 4 by 12 feet should be allowed for each man.

Uprights of 4 by 4 stuff, projecting 8 feet above the platform and carrying a crosspiece sufficiently long to project at least a foot beyond the outer edge of the platform, should be erected at intervals of 12 feet. These uprights, with their crosspieces, provide the support for the swimmer and they must, therefore, be securely bolted to the face of the dock and to the sleepers of the platform, and the crosspiece, which has a swivel pulley large enough to take the swimming-rope attached to the outer end, must be braced against the upright. Ladders leading to the platform from the water should be placed where they will not be in the way.

2. Where it is impracticable to build the platform described above, the uprights alone will answer the purpose of instructing the men in the stroke, swimming poles being used when the soldier is able to propel himself.

3. The simplest device, in connection with giving this instruction from the dock, consists in erecting an upright about 42 inches high

close to the edge of the dock, and use it as a fulcrum for the swimming pole, the soldier being suspended from a rope attached to the end of the pole.

4. When no docks are available, platforms along the lines described under 1 may be erected in the water on piles or, when this is impracticable, floats with raised platforms and uprights may be substituted.

8. In the absence of any facilities, but where the character of the water and the bottom is such as to make it possible, the men must be instructed to assist one another. This is done by standing in water of sufficient depth and holding the one to be instructed in the proper position by placing the left hand under his chin and the right hand between his shoulder blades and assuming a position that will not interfere with the swimmer's movements.

BELTS.

6. These are 3 inches wide, made of canvas, padded on the inside with hair and bound and faced with some soft material that will not irritate the skin. The length should be great enough to bring the ends of the belt to within 4 inches of meeting in the back.

On the outside of the belt three ¾-inch iron rings are securely sewed to it at regular intervals, while at each end of the belt there is a larger ring 1 inch in diameter.

ROPES.

7. A half inch cotton rope should be used; for beginners 15 feet will be found ample, while 30 feet should be used for those preparing to qualify.

ROPES AND BELTS.

8. The rope should be fastened in the following manner: Tie the end of the rope securely to the small ring, 1, nearest the larger one, A; pass it through the other two small rings, 2 and 3, and through the two larger ones, B and A; then through B, forward, and then

SWIMMING.   317

halfway between A and B, where it is looped and passed under. Plate A.

The advantage of this arrangement is its safety, the rope can not become untied; it is readily adjusted; all that is necessary is to loosen the loop and pull the ends of the belt apart; once it is adjusted to the swimmer it remains fixed, there is no tightening due to slipping on account of the weight thrown upon it.

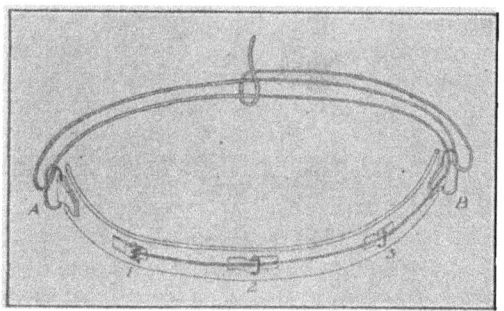

PLATE A.

POLES.

9. These should be of some tough, but light, material, 2 inches in diameter and from 8 to 10 feet long. At one end a swivel pulley is attached through which the swimming rope is run.

In the absence of projecting swimming platforms, beginners are suspended from the end of these poles resting on the upright fulcrum described under 3, until they have acquired the stroke. When they begin to make progress and are propelling themselves, the instructor carries the pole in his hands with the end projecting far enough over the edge of the dock to give the swimmer sufficient space to move in without coming in contact with the dock.

INSTRUCTION.

THE BREAST STROKE.

10. This stroke having for many years been found the best adapted for military purposes, has been adopted by all armies in which the instruction in swimming is made compulsory.

It is the basis upon which all other methods of progression in the water are founded, and those who acquire proficiency in its use develop coordination to such a degree that they have no difficulty whatever in acquiring any other stroke, no matter how complicated.

The character of the movements comprising this stroke brings into play such a great variety of muscle groups, all in accordance with their natural functions and with such an equal distribution of effort, that aside from its usefulness this stroke has an incomparable value as an agent for all-around development.

LAND INSTRUCTION.

11. The efficacy of this instruction is a mooted question; and experience has demonstrated that aside from giving the beginner a conception of what is required of him when he enters the water it is of little value; in other words, swimming instruction in order to be successful must be imparted to the beginner while he is in the water.

Various methods are used for swimming instruction on land, and some of them are noted here for the benefit of those who desire to make use of them.

The appliance most commonly used is the so-called "swimming buck," a camp stool slightly wider and higher than the ordinary one, upon which the beginner assumes a position in every way similar to that assumed in the water. The instruction proceeds in indentically the same way as that described in the water instruction.

Another method is to lie on the back in a position that approximates as closely as possible to the first position in the water instruction and execute the movements in that position.

Still another method is to stand on one leg, supporting the body with the hand on the same side, and with the body bent forward horizontally and the other arm and leg extended to the front and rear, respectively, execute the movements with one side several times and then repeat it with the other.

WATER INSTRUCTION.

12. The belt having been adjusted, which is done by slipping it over the head of the soldier and securing it well up under his arms, being careful not to have it so tight that it will bind his movements or restrict his respiration, and being careful also that the loop of the rope is squarely between the shoulder blades, he is prepared to leap into the water. This should always be insisted upon, since, while it appears drastic, it is most efficacious in overcoming the fear of the water so common amongst adults who have not learned how to swim.

The soldier having been cautioned not to gasp or open his mouth when he strikes the water and not to throw his arms about wildly, but to *open his eyes* and to *keep cool*, leaps from the platform at the command *Jump*, which is executed with the feet striking the water first, legs together and extended, trunk erect, and arms at the sides.

After reaching the surface, in which he is assisted by the instructor, he will assume the following position:

The body, chest down, is fully extended horizontally; the head is bent back; the arms, with fingers extended and closed and thumbs together and palms down, are stretched to the front, hands just under the surface; the legs, with knees straight, are closed and extended horizontally to the rear; the heels are together and the feet are turned out at an angle of about 60° and the toes are turned up perpendicular to the surface. Fig. 1.

In assuming this position care should be taken to avoid any tendency toward rigidity; the muscles are stretched, not contracted.

In this position the instructor commands:

1. Arm Stroke, 2. ONE, 3. TWO, 4. THREE.

At *one*, the arms fully stretched, palms down, are moved sideward horizontally, in a circular motion of greatest possible radius until they are in a line with the shoulders.

At *two*, the elbows are flexed until the upper arms touch and are parallel to the chest, the forearms, palms still turned down, continue the motion until the thumbs are brought together directly under the chin.

At *three*, the arms are stretched forward to the original position, Fig. 1.

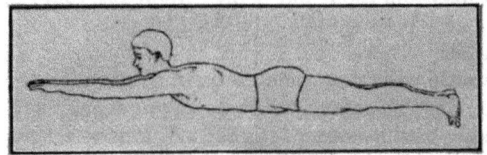

FIG. 1.

In the beginning a pause should be made in every position to insure accuracy; when that has been attained the arm stroke is executed in one continuous movement in the following manner:

At *o-n-e*, drawn out to indicate the character of the movement, which is comparatively slow, the arms are brought in line with the shoulders, as described before; the moment that movement is about to be completed the command *and—two* is given, briskly followed by the command *three*. At *and—two*, the arms are drawn to the body and extended forward, in a continuous movement; and at *three*, the arms pause in the first position.

The cadence indicated here is the regular swimming cadence, the first count requiring as much time as the others combined.

The legs may be relaxed while the arms are being exercised.

SWIMMING.

Proper breathing is always a source of considerable annoyance to beginners, and instructors can not begin too early to teach how and when to inhale and to exhale. This should be done when the arm stroke is taught and insisted upon throughout the instruction until respiration is carried on naturally. The inhalation occurs while the arms are being moved outward and sideward, and the exhalation follows immediately after their extension. In quiet water this breathing may be carried on through the nostrils, but in rough water or where there is a tendency to choke because of water entering the nostrils, mouth breathing must be resorted to.

When the arm movements are understood and accurately performed the instructor will command:

1. Leg Stroke, 2. ONE, 3. TWO, 4. THREE.

The arms are held in the forward position without constraint.

At *one*, the legs and thighs are flexed on the body by drawing the knees under it until the thighs are slightly beyond the perpendicular and the legs horizontal; the heels remain together, the toes turned out and up, but the knees are separated, being in line with the feet.

At *two*, the legs are quickly and fully extended in as wide a straddle as possible with an outward and backward motion, the soles of the feet being forced against the water.

At *three*, the legs, remaining fully extended, are brought together briskly to the first position.

As in the arm stroke, a pause should be made in each position to insure accuracy, and when that has been accomplished the leg movements should be blended into one continuous motion as follows:

At *one*, the legs remain in the first position; and at *and*, they are drawn up as described above, the movement being executed quietly and without force in order to avoid offering too much resistance to the water; just as the legs reach the prescribed position the commands *two* and *three* are given briskly and in quick succession, indicating that the completion of sideward movement is followed instantly by the closing of the legs.

When these movements are thoroughly understood and correctly carried out, the arm and leg movements are combined and executed at the command:

1. Stroke, 2. ONE, 3. AND—TWO, 4. THREE.

At *one*, the arms begin the sideward movement, the legs remaining in the first position.

At *and*, the arms are drawn in to the body and the knees are brought up. Fig. 2.

At *two*, the arms are extended forward and the legs sideward, Fig. 3; and at *three*, the legs are closed, while the arms remain in the first position. Fig. 1.

FIG. 2.

Until the soldier has learned to coordinate and to grasp what is required of him, it is advisable to pause in each position; when he has succeeded in doing this the stroke is given in the proper swimming cadence, the arm movements beginning at *one* and ceasing at *two* and pausing at *three;* while the legs remain motionless in the first position at *one*, but begin at *and* and cease at *three;* a considerable pause should be made between strokes.

It is advisable to impress upon beginners that swimming with this stroke is not dependent upon excessive muscular exertion or rigidity, but that all extensions of the arms and legs are reaches rather than thrusts, and that the body must be relaxed as much as possible.

Since there is no danger of the body sinking while it is moving, too much stress can hardly be laid upon the importance of the pause between strokes, which in the case of even ordinary swimmers should be equal to the length of time it takes to complete the stroke, while in powerful swimmers this pause is from three to four times the duration of each stroke, a husbanding of muscular energy which makes it possible to swim long distances without becoming exhausted.

The men must also be given to understand that the *legs furnish the entire propelling power* in which the closing of the legs after the

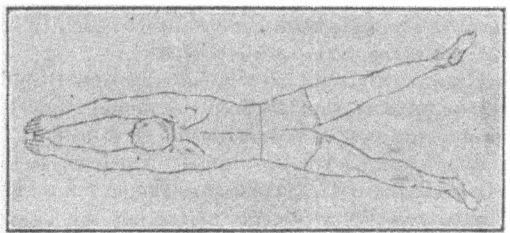

FIG. 3.

extension is equally as valuable as the extension itself. The arms, for ordinary purposes, are used merely for the purpose of buoying up the head, not for the purpose of propulsion, and for that reason they are held and moved in a position that has the advantage of being the most natural, the least fatiguing, and that offers the least resistance to the water. Thus the entire burden of the effort devolves upon those members of the body upon which this burden is imposed upon the land, *the legs*, and not upon those members which nature never intended for such a purpose, *the arms*. It is due entirely to this natural and equable employment of those members that the breast stroke is used, without exception almost, by all long-distance swimmers when it is a question of endurance rather than of speed. For the latter purpose the hands may be turned with the palms out in the first motion, but this should be restricted to those who have qualified with the regular stroke, and who appreciate the value of the leg stroke.

When the soldier can execute the movements faultlessly and without the numbers, he is released from further instruction on the stationary line and given instruction on a loose line. The belt, being adjusted as before, is attached to a line that is held in the hands of the instructor. The man now begins the stroke at one end of the platform and as he forces himself forward the instructor advances with him, having the rope taut and standing while the pupil is bringing his arms around and his knees up and slightly slackening the rope and advancing a step as he extends.

In a short time he will begin to carry his own weight, and when he has learned to swim from 30 to 50 strokes he should be made to swim on the arch of a circle whose radius should be constantly increased until he is able to swim several minutes. When he can do this he should be timed daily until he is able to swim for ten minutes, when he should be excused from further instruction, but encouraged to continue practice daily until he has gained confidence in himself and learned to keep himself afloat by other methods besides the breast stroke.

COMMON FAULTS.

13. For the benefit of instructors, the faults and bad habits most common with beginners are enumerated here:

The tendency to arch the back in order to raise the head higher above the water than necessary: This causes the body to be held in a constraint position and the legs to sink, thereby presenting a greater resistive surface to the water, causing slow and deep swimming. The body must be relaxed and if necessary the chin may rest upon the surface of the water; this will cause the legs to rise.

Raising the hips while drawing the knees up: This causes the head to be thrown forward into the water and detracts from the power of the leg motions.

Not flexing the thighs sufficiently, which causes the feet to assume a horizontal instead of a perpendicular position, thereby not only decreasing the sideward reach of the leg stroke but also the power of the backward push with the soles of the feet.

Thrusting the arms forward below the horizontal, thereby lessening the buoyancy of the head which is dragged downward by this movement.

Failure to draw the upper arms in close to the chin and the hands under the chin, which serves to decrease the buoyancy of the upper trunk and head.

Thrusting the legs downward instead of straight to the rear, which causes deep swimming and impedes progress.

Spreading the fingers and failing to keep the thumb close to the first finger, which detracts very decidedly from the buoyance power of the arms and hands.

Not breathing properly, which causes mental anxiety, fatigue, and respiratory difficulties.

Moving the arms too far to the rear, which causes the head to be lowered.

Disregarding the tempo of the stroke and the pause between the strokes, which always results in loss of confidence and of the stroke.

SIDE STROKE.

14. Those who have acquired proficiency in the breast stroke, will, as has been stated before, have no difficulty in mastering any other method, by dint of a little practice and perseverance, regular instruction being unnecessary.

The *side stroke* is readily learned, and since it can be carried out on either side it has many advantages over the one-sided methods.

326 MANUAL OF PHYSICAL TRAINING.

The swimmer lies upon his side, preferably the right, the head, face turned upward, resting in the water; the body and legs extended without constraint and the right arm stretched straight out under the head in prolongation of the body; the left arm stretched downward over the left thigh with the hand just in rear of the body; palms of both hands down. Fig. 4.

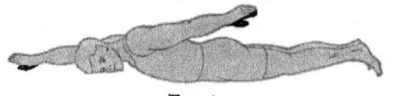

FIG. 4.

From this position the left forearm is brought up across the chest until the hand, palm down, is close to the chin; the right arm in the meanwhile is pressed downward about 45°, when the elbow is bent and drawn back under the chest until the hand, palm down, is as close as possible to the right shoulder. While the arms are executing

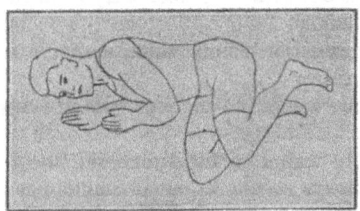

FIG. 5.

these movements, the knees are drawn up precisely as they are in the breast stroke, Fig. 5. From this position the legs are extended and closed as in the breast stroke, except that they are not so far apart, and the arms are extended, Fig. 6, the right straight out under the head to its original position and the left arm forward and then backward in as large a circular sweep as possible until it, too, reaches its original position, Fig. 4. After pausing, the length of the pause depending upon the carrying quality of the stroke, the movement is repeated.

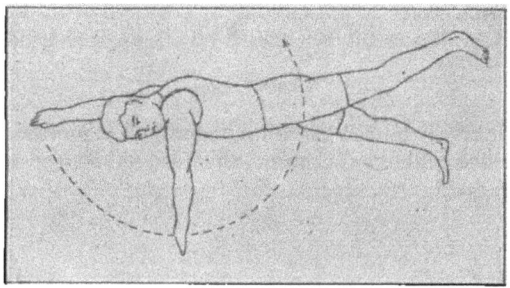

Fig. 6.

Fig. 7.

Variety may be given this stroke by the introduction of the "scissors kick," the upper leg being extended straight out to the front and the under leg to the rear, the legs being brought to the first position from there. Figs. 7 and 8.

BACK STROKE.

15. As the body displaces more water when lying on the back than it does in any other position, thus increasing its buoyancy, swimming with the back stroke is the most easily acquired of any stroke. Its greatest value lies in the fact that it affords an exhausted swimmer a chance to rest.

1. *With legs.*

The swimmer extends himself in the water, face upward, body and legs extended without constraint; the head submerged to the ears

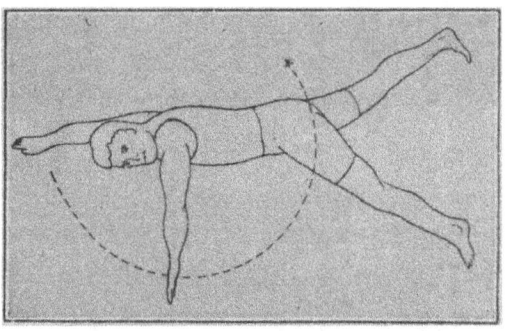

Fig. 8.

and the arms lying close to the sides, palms down. In this position he executes the leg movements of the breast stroke, except that the knees are not drawn up as high and are separated more. Care should be taken not to move the hips while the knees are being drawn up and extended, because any motion of the hips will cause the head to be submerged.

2. *With legs and arms.*

The position is the same as above. When the knees are being drawn up, the elbows are bent and raised until the upper arms are in line with the shoulders, and the hands, palms down, are close to the chest; as the knees are being extended and the legs closed, the arms are flung out sideward and brought down to the sides in a whip-like movement, the palms turned in.

3. *With legs and overhead arm stroke.*

In this stroke the arms are raised forward and overhead, out of the water, and as they enter the water beyond the head they are brought to the sides of the body with a strong horizontal movement, arms extended and palms down. The knees are drawn up just as the arms enter the water, and they are extended and closed while the arms are being brought to the sides.

TREADING WATER.

16. The body is held in a perpendicular position and the knees are drawn up and extended downward alternately in quick succession, the hands assisting by pressing the water downward.

Treading water may also be done by executing the leg motions of the breast stroke in a modified form in quick succession. These movements should be practiced until the swimmer is able to raise his hands out of water.

FLOATING.

17. Floating is essential because it affords the swimmer the most complete rest in the water, thus giving him an opportunity to repair his strength.

In fresh water this means of sustaining the body is possible only in exceptional cases with men; in salt water, however, the inability to float is the exception.

The swimmer lies in the water horizontally, face up, exerting himself just enough to keep his body, arms, and legs fully but not rigidly extended. The whole body, except the face and mouth, should be submerged. The legs may be kept closed or separated; the arms should be held away from the body, hands in the plane of the waist with the palms down; the lungs should be inflated and by short exhalations and proportionately longer inhalation, carried on through the mouth, they should be kept so as much as possible.

When difficulty is encountered in floating, a slight sculling movement of the hands, from the wrist, will often suffice to keep the body afloat. If the legs should sink, they may be held flexed at the knees until they are at right angles to the thighs; or the body may be "dished" slightly; that is, bent slightly forward at the waist.

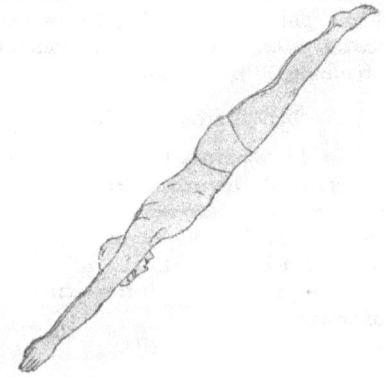

FIG. 9.

DIVING.

18. This may be divided into the ordinary dive, in which the body enters the water at an angle of 45°; the perpendicular, or deep dive, and the shallow dive, in which the body enters the water at an angle of about 30°, Figs. 9, 10, and 11.

In preparing to dive the swimmer stands with his toes projecting beyond the edge of the platform and his arms stretched sideward. As he springs off, the arms are swung forward overhead, palms together; the head is thrown forward between the arms and the legs are swung up until the body assumes the desired angle. Arms and legs must be extended and closed, feet depressed. The moment

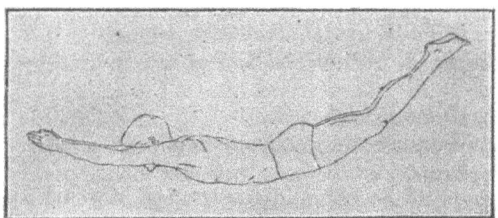

Fig. 10.

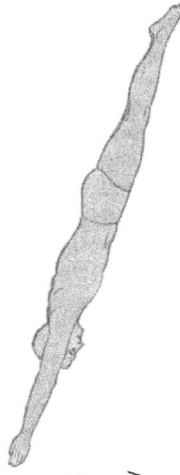

Fig. 11.

the body enters the water the eyes are opened, the arms and head pressed back, and the legs relaxed; this will cause the body to rise to the surface.

SWIMMING WITH EQUIPMENT.

19. When the men become proficient swimmers they should be taught to swim with the equipment.

This instruction should be divided as follows:

1. Swimming in uniform; if blouses are worn they should be unbuttoned.
2. Swimming nude with pack.
3. Swimming nude with pack and ammunition belt.
4. Swimming nude with pack, belt, and rifle.

> The pack should be adjusted to the body snugly to reduce the lateral motion as much as possible; the canteen should be empty and the rifle should be inserted into the middle of the pack, barrel down, until the breech mechanism projects over the water.

5. Repeat 2, 3, and 4, clad in trousers.
6. Same, clad in trousers and shirts.
7. Same, in complete uniform.

Except when the urgency of the emergency does not permit it, the men should be permitted to divest themselves of their shoes, leggins and blouses and attach them to the pack.

Since the buoyance and water-tightness of the packs is great enough to keep them afloat from 15 to 20 minutes, they lend themselves admirably to the formation of rafts, when fastened together, to which those who can not swim can cling while being drawn over a stream by a rope, one end of which has been carried over by a swimmer.

GENERAL HINTS.

1. Swimming should not be indulged in immediately before or after meals, the best time being an hour before or from two to three hours after meals.

2. The water should not be entered when the body is overheated or wet with perspiration; cramps or other more serious discomforts are likely to result.

SWIMMING.

3. The body should be dried thoroughly and the water should be entered by plunging in head foremost, if practicable, or by leaping.

4. Men should be cautioned not to stand in the water to cool off, as doing so has an enervating effect.

5. While in the water the body should be kept in motion; standing about after swimming is liable to cause chills.

6. When through swimming the water should be quitted at once and the body dried and dressed promptly.

7. During instructions only those that are employed should leave the dressing rooms; when it is necessary to have more men than can be employed on the platform, those not employed should be made to wear blouses or other covering for the body.

8. When attacked by cramps the men should be instructed not to lose presence of mind, but to kick out more vigorously than ever if a leg is affected; if an arm, they should turn over on the back and swim with the leg stroke, in the meantime rubbing the affected arm vigorously.

9. The undertaking of hazardous ventures for the sake of display should meet the unqualified condemnation of those in charge of this instruction, since many fatalities are directly traceable to such foolhardiness.

10. Lack of confidence is never overcome by drastic measures or ridicule; gentleness and perseverance will be found much more efficacious. Fearsomeness while in the water is usually not due to cowardliness but to a lack of confidence or to an inherent fear over which many who do not lack bravery in other things have no control.

11. Going to the assistance of a drowning man is at best a very precarious undertaking and should, therefore, be limited to those who are cool-headed and strong swimmers.

12. In approaching a man in danger extreme caution should be exercised lest he grab his would-be rescuer. The approach should be from the left and rear, leaving the right arm of the rescuer free for defensive purposes in case he should be clutched. The helpless

man's upper arms should be firmly gripped and he should be pulled over on his back, the rescuer, too, turning on his back and towing the other in by using the backstroke. The men should be instructed in this method, using each other as subjects.

13. In an extremity, when a rescuer finds his life is being endangered, he should not hesitate to resort to extreme measures of self-defense, such as striking with the fist between the eyes, choking, or submerging the head of him to whose rescue he has gone. Restoration to consciousness is readily accomplished, if unconsciousness has resulted from this treatment, once land has been reached.

RESTORATION OF THOSE APPARENTLY DEAD FROM DROWNING.

As soon as the body has been recovered, resuscitation should, if the weather is not inclement, be attempted on the spot.

1. Remove all the clothing from the patient's chest.

2. Place him on the ground, face down, and grasp him under the abdomen and raise him up. This will give the water he has swallowed an opportunity to escape and free the air passages.

3. Turn the patient over, and with a handkerchief wrapped around the first finger clean the mouth and nostrils.

4. *Draw out the tongue* and hold it in that position by an elastic band, string, tape, or a strip of cloth torn from a handkerchief; or have an assistant hold it with his fingers wrapped in a handkerchief or cloth.

5. Use the following method of artificial respiration, which is known as the Sylvester method:

Place the patient on his back and lay a roll of clothing, coat, or other garment under his shoulders. This roll must be large enough to raise the shoulders and throw the head slightly to the rear.

6. Kneel at his head and grasp his arms, one in each hand, with fingers out and thumb in, just below the elbows, and draw the arms outward, away from the chest, till they meet overhead. *This*

movement imitates inspiration. The arms are then turned down and forcibly pressed against the chest for a moment. *This movement imitates expiration.* Continue these movements perseveringly at the rate of about 15 times per minute until signs of natural respiration are perceived.

7. While those movements are going on, the clothing remaining on the patient should be removed by an assistant, *without interfering with the artificial respiration*, however. When the body is stripped it should be dried and covered with such clothing as may be available.

8. An attempt to produce natural respiration by exciting the respiratory nerves may also be made by holding ammonia to the nostrils, by slapping the chest alternately with cloths wrung out in hot and cold water, or by tickling the nostrils with a feather.

9. When breathing has been restored, the limbs of the patient should be rubbed upward, toward the heart, vigorously in order to restore the circulation. The rubbing should be done under the covering as much as possible, and in order to restore the warmth of the body extra covering, hot flannels, bricks, or bottles should be applied.

10. To stimulate the vital organs, small doses of aromatic spirits of ammonia should be given.

O

A Selection Of Classic Instructive Titles Relating To
The Art Of Pugilism & Self Defence
In Both War & Peace
Find our entire selection @ naval-military-press.com

ALL-IN FIGHTING
The distilled knowledge of W.E. Fairbairn, legendary SOE instructor in unarmed combat, and inventor of the Sykes-Fairbairn knife, who learned his deadly skills in 30 years on the Shanghai waterfront.
Fully illustrated.
9781847348531

ART OF BOXING AND SCIENCE OF SELF DEFENCE
Former Lightweight Champion Billy Edwards shares the techniques and strategies of the sweet science in his beautifully illustrated boxing guide. Explore boxing's transition from bare knuckle spectacle to today's Marquis of Queensbury ruleset.
9781474539548

SELF DEFENCE OR THE ART OF BOXING
Ned Donnelly was a pioneer of boxing training during the late Victorian era. Explore the strategies and techniques used by this trainer of champions via a series of easy-to-follow illustrations and clear, concise coaching steps.
9781474539562

ART OF WRESTLING
George de Relwyskow Army Gymnastic Staff
In the appreciation to this book Captain Daniels, V.C., M.C., Rifle Brigade, states: "In adding a word to this book on the style of wrestling as taught at the Headquarters Gymnasium of the British Army, and having had personal experience in the various holds and throws taught, I consider it has been of great value in the training of the soldier, and the bringing out of those qualities of grit and determination which have been seen in all ranks who have taken an active part throughout the greatest war in history." 1919.
9781783313563

THE COMPLETE BOXER
Gunner Moir provides detailed instructions on the techniques he deployed to become British Heavyweight Champion. Taught in a series of easy to learn techniques, combinations, and boxing strategies.
9781474539609

BOXING (V-Five)
The Aviation Training Office of the Chief of Naval Operations
The game-changing V-Five suite of training manuals helped get a generation of American aviators fit for war. Here we explore how the airmen of the US navy trained in boxing as part of their military fitness regime.
9781474539623

WRESTLING (V-Five)
The Aviation Training Office of the Chief of Naval Operations
The game-changing V-Five suite of training manuals helped get a generation of American aviators fit for war. Here we explore how the airmen of the US navy trained in collegiate wrestling as part of their military fitness regime.
9781474539685

THE TEXTBOOK OF WRESTLING
Get your wrestling skills matt-ready from wrestling champion and world-renown trainer Ernest Gruhn. Replete with detailed holds, throws, pins and strategies for success in a wide range of wrestling rulesets.
9781474539647

KILL OR GET KILLED
Rex Applegate's "kill or be killed" helped prepare America's marines, soldiers, sailors, spies and airmen for the realities of war. This highly shared and respected work provides all you need to know about unarmed combat and close quarter engagement with the enemy.
9781474539661

JACK GOODWIN'S BOXING
This 1920's boxing masterpiece by Jack Goodwin puts you in the shoes of a coach in that era. Uncover the best ways to run, manage and train boxers as taught by Jack Goodwin, a champion and trainer of champions in the noble science.
9781474539586

DEAL THE FIRST DEADLY BLOW
United States Department of the Army

This Vietnam-era classic showcases in detail how the US Forces trained in close quarter combat. Known as the "encyclopaedia of combat" it helped a generation learn how to become devastating effective with empty hands, knives and bayonets alike.

9781474539722

HAND-TO-HAND COMBAT
Bureau of Aeronautics U.S Navy 1943

This is one of the best combative manuals from World War 2, developed by the US Navy V-Five Staff, that included the renowned American wrestler Wesley Brown. It is then not especially surprising that wrestling skills predominate in this manual, and form the base skill-set for this combative system.

9781474537391

ABWEHR ENGLISCHER GANGSTER METHODEN DEFENSE OF ENGLISH GANGSTERS METHODS – SILENT KILLING – FULL ENGLISH TRANSLATION

In 1942 the Wehrmacht published a training manual with the goal of countering the "silent killing" tactics used by the British commando units. The manual was – much in line with typical National Socialist terminology –titled

"Abwehr Englischer Gangster-methoden" or "Defence Against English Gangster methods".

This book was compiled due the Wehrmacht intelligence operatives uncovering of a British hand-to-hand course for the SOE, Commandos, et al, on methods of quick and silent killing (undoubtedly developed by W. E. Fairbairn and E. A. Sykes). They correctly assessed that their troops in general and particularly the Geheime Staatspolizei (Gestapo), Sicherheitsdienst (SD), their security guards, and sentries would be in grave danger when confronted by men trained in these methods. This manual/program was the Wehrmacht's response.

9781474538336

HAND TO HAND COMBAT

Francois d'Eliscu taught thousands of U.S. Army Rangers how to fight down and dirty in World War II.d'Eliscu doesn't get the press that Fairbairn and Applegate do, but he did a commendable job writing this book.It is basic, meant for training raw recruits in a short amount of time before sending them to the front, but simple is good when you are in combat, as most combative experts' will tell you.

9781474535823

W.E Fairbairn's Complete Compendium of Lethal, Unarmed, Hand-to-Hand Combat Methods and Fighting In Colour

All 844 images of Fairbairn and his assistants can now for the first time be seen in full colour, lending a clarity to the practical methods of mastering the manner of dealing with an assailant, both in time of war and when placed in difficulty during unpleasant modern urban situations. These various holds, trips, kicks, blows etc, allow the average man or woman a position of security against almost any form of armed or unarmed attack.

Captain W.E. Fairbairn would have approved of this new colour version, that gives an illustrative clarity to the original that was lacking in previous monochrome reprints of his work.

All six of W.E. Fairbairn's works in one binding to create the ultimate colour compendium: Get Tough-All-In Fighting-Shooting to Live-Scientific Self-Defence-Hands Off!-Defendu

9781783318735

BOXING FOR BOYS
Regtl. Sergt.-Major & B Dent Army Gymnastic Headquarters
A successful system of boxing instruction for large classes, to allow tuition with no detriment to the "backward or shy pupil". Covers Kit-On, Guard-Sparring-Advance-Point & Mark-Ducking-Medicine, Bag-Left & Right Hooks etc. The author considered that boxing systematically taught to the youth was beneficial exercise, and would have a marked elevating influence on the national character.
9781783314607

HAND-TO-HAND FIGHTING
A System Of Personal Defence For The Soldier (1918)
A tough book on the art of hand to hand fighting in the trenches of the Great War. Demonstrating techniques utilised to "do away with the enemy", many of which are barred in clean wrestling, the book includes good clear photographic illustrations presenting important attack methods including the "Hammer Lock", "Kidney Kick", "Head Twist", "Knee Groin Kick", and the "Knee Break", all very important in a man to man, life or death encounter, when fighting in the mud of the trenches.
9781783313983

www.ingramcontent.com/pod-product-compliance
Lightning Source LLC
Chambersburg PA
CBHW070735170426
43200CB00007B/528